Teddy Bears
Forever!

Dedicated to all Teddy Bears — past, present and future

Published by David Bateman Ltd
32–34 View Road
Glenfield, Auckland
New Zealand

This edition published in 1988 by Tiger Books International Ltd., London.

A David Bateman Book
Designed by Bruce Dimond, Mary Harris
Typeset in Auckland, New Zealand by Lazerprintz
Printed in Hong Kong by Mandarin Offset

ISBN 1-870461-55-X

Teddy Bears Forever!

Stories by Barbara Hayes
Illustrated by John King

TIGER BOOKS INTERNATIONAL
LONDON

Dear Readers,

When I was little, my auntie gave me a very large teddy bear which she had won in a raffle from a corner shop. He was a clever teddy with a good memory. He told me a lot of things about Teddy Bear Land and he passed on a lot of stories he had overheard in the shop, while he was waiting for the raffle to be drawn.

Many years later, when I had children of my own, a white teddy called Snowy Bear was given to my son. Snowy was a polar bear who had travelled all round about the North Pole and he told us lots of exciting tales about what went on in those wild, dangerous places.

In this book I have written, as well as I can remember them, the stories the teddy bears told to us. I hope you enjoy them as much as we did.

With best wishes to you all,

Barbara Hayes

Contents

TOYLAND
ROSEBUD

Leaving Teddy Bear Land

Far, far away in the heart of a thick forest is Teddy Bear Land. It is a beautiful place, for generations of bears have cleared the trees away and built cosy houses and planted pretty gardens. Some bears live all their lives in Teddy Bear Land. Other bears, especially the young adventurous ones, like to set off to see the great wide world. Some of these bears go to Fairytale Land and have adventures there. Others make the dangerous journey by sledge through the thick, snowy forest to Father Christmas Land. There they help get everything ready for the Christmas delivery of themselves and the other toys. Most of the bears make arrangements to go by coach along the Forest Highway to the toy shops.

Not very long ago a young, golden-coloured teddy decided that it was time to set off to see the world.

"I have done all my training," Young Golden Teddy smiled to himself. "I can count to one hundred. I have good table manners. I know the polite way to behave and I know that the most important thing for any teddy bear is to be a LOYAL FRIEND."

Young Golden Teddy's smile suddenly faltered.

"Of course, I wasn't good at learning to tell the time," he muttered. "I still get muddled about which is three o'clock and which is nine o'clock, and I am never absolutely certain when the time is six o'clock or half past twelve. However," he lifted his chin defiantly, "I did well in all the important subjects, and if I was bottom of the class in telling the time, well, nobody is perfect."

Young Golden Bear hurried into the house of Red Tape Bear who made all the arrangements for the bears who wanted to leave Teddy Bear Land. Red Tape Bear was called Red Tape because his jacket was decorated with red tape round the collars and cuffs, and because he kept all his papers and files in tidy bundles wound round and round with miles more of the same red tape.

"So you want to go out into the great wide world," said Red Tape Bear. "I am sure that can be arranged if we fill in the right form."

He took down a neat bundle from a shelf and spent ten minutes unwinding the red tape.

"I hate to interfere," said Young Golden Bear, "and I only ask in order to improve my knowledge, but why do you wind so much red tape round the bundle of forms? You could keep the bundle equally as tidy with one short length of tape and you could untie it in ten seconds instead of ten minutes."

Red Tape Bear looked at Young Golden Bear in astonishment.

"I love red tape," he replied. "It is impossible to have too much red tape. I come to my office to play with the red tape. I fit in making the arrangements for you young bears as an extra job and out of the kindness of my heart — and don't you forget it."

"Oh indeed! In that case thank you very much," said Young Golden Bear, trying to feel grateful.

Red Tape Bear finally finished unwinding the red tape. "Here we are!" he smiled at last, finding the form. "Now, do you want to go to Fairytale Land for adventures, or do you want to go to Father Christmas Land? Or do you want to go to the shops and wait for a boy or girl to choose you as a loyal friend?"

Young Golden Bear did not hesitate. "I want to go to the

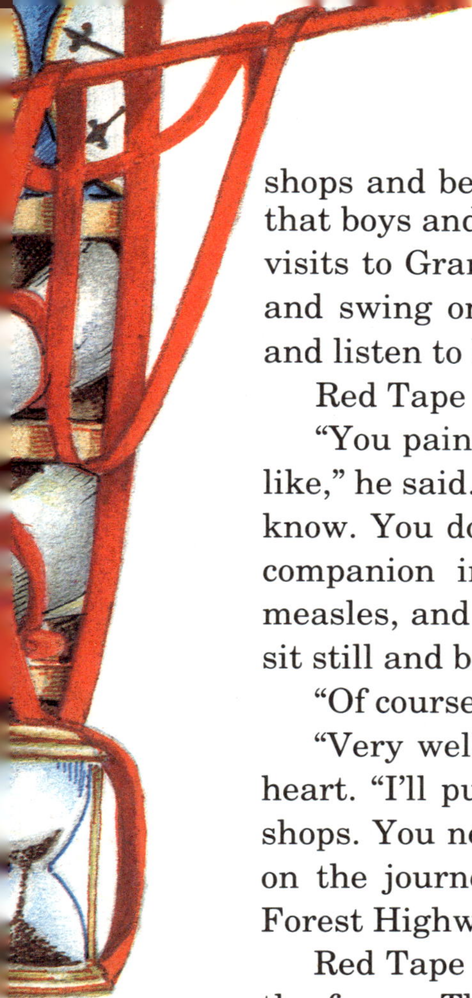

shops and become a loyal friend," he said firmly. "I have heard that boys and girls take their teddies to the supermarket and on visits to Grandma and Grandpa. They go for walks in the park and swing on swings. Teddies are allowed to watch television and listen to bedtime stories. It all sounds marvellous to me."

Red Tape Bear looked hard at Young Golden Bear.

"You paint a very rosy picture of what being a loyal friend is like," he said. "Life in the great wide world has its hard side, you know. You do understand that it is a teddy bear's duty to be a companion in good times and bad, during chicken-pox and measles, and cutting double teeth, and while your owner has to sit still and be good when important visitors are in the house."

"Of course!" agreed Young Golden Bear. "And I will do it too."

"Very well," smiled Red Tape Bear, who was a good sort at heart. "I'll put your name down to go on the next coach to the shops. You need no luggage. Drinks and meals will be provided on the journey. Be at the coach stop at the beginning of the Forest Highway at fifteen hundred hours. Next."

Red Tape Bear started to rewind all the red tape back round the forms. The young blue teddy who was waiting next in line leant forward and said, "There's no need to wind that red tape back. I want you to fill out one of those forms for me. If you wind the tape back on, you will only have to unwind it again, and all that will make twenty minutes of unnecessary work."

Red Tape Bear beamed. "I know! I know!" he smiled. "But what fun!"

Suddenly Red Tape Bear and the blue teddy noticed that Young Golden Bear was still in the room.

"Why are you waiting?" asked Red Tape Bear. His eyes suddenly glistened happily. "Do you want me to fill in another form?"

"No thank you," said Young Golden Teddy. "I didn't understand what you said about the time to meet the coach."

"Fifteen hundred hours!" repeated Red Tape Bear. "FIFTEEN HUNDRED HOURS," he said again in a louder voice, as Young Golden Bear continued to look blank. Then he added, "You are too young to be going deaf, aren't you? I say, YOU ARE YOUNG TO BE GOING DEAF!"

Young Golden Bear clutched at his ears. "There is no need to

13:7
BEARN

shout," he growled. "I am not going deaf, but I don't understand what fifteen hundred hours means. I know I was not good at learning to tell the time, but I distinctly remember hearing the teacher say that there are twelve hours in the day and twenty-four hours in day and night put together, so where do these hundreds of hours come from?"

Blue Teddy was a good-natured fellow and he tried to help. "You say things like fifteen hundred hours when you are using what is called a twenty-four-hour clock," he explained. "Really you mean fifteen hours, but you put two noughts after the fifteen to show there are no minutes and call it fifteen hundred hours because that is what you have written. It is a clever idea to stop you from getting into a muddle between day and night."

Young Golden Teddy stared back in surprise.

"How can anyone get in a muddle between day and night?" he asked. "During the day it is light and during the night it is dark. I don't need any twenty-four-hour clock to tell me that."

"No, no," went on Blue Teddy. "Fifteen hundred hours in twenty-four-hour clock language means three o'clock in the afternoon. You see, there are two three o'clocks. There is three o'clock in the very, very early morning, soon after midnight, when it is still dark, and there is three o'clock in the afternoon. Supposing Red Tape Bear had said to you, catch the coach at three o'clock, you might have gone to the coach stop at three o'clock in the morning."

"No I should not!" replied Young Golden Teddy. "At three o'clock in the morning I am in bed asleep, like every other sensible person."

He glanced from Red Tape Bear to Blue Teddy.

"I thought trying to learn the difference between three o'clock and nine o'clock, and six o'clock and half-past twelve, was bad enough," he said, "but now you are making my heard whirl with twenty-four-hour clocks which have hundreds of hours in them. Well, I tell you, I don't believe a word of it. I will catch that coach in my own way and it will be a better way than trying to fill my head with all this time nonsense."

Young Golden Teddy, who could be quite a fierce little teddy when he felt like it, stomped out of the room. He went to the cake shop and bought a bag of buns. He bought a bottle of lemonade.

He bought a good book. He walked down to the beginning of the Forest Highway, which led from Teddy Bear Land through the thick forest into the great wide world. He sat on the bench at the side of the coach stop. Young Golden Teddy had a marvellous time eating the buns and drinking the lemonade and reading the book. He chatted to everyone who passed by and they all wished him luck in his new life as a loyal friend.

"As long as I am sitting here, whenever the coach arrives at whatever time of day or night, I shall be ready to catch it," smiled Young Golden Teddy. "This is much better than giving myself a headache bothering with all those muddling hours."

Eventually the coach arrived and Young Golden Teddy climbed aboard. He sat in a comfortable seat and had an interesting journey looking out through the window all the way to a fine toy shop.

After a while Young Golden Teddy sent word back to Teddy Bear Land that he had become a loyal friend to a girl named Jane, who was wonderful at telling the time.

"I never have to bother with trying to tell the time," said Young Golden Teddy in his message. "Everything has worked out perfectly."

As indeed it had!

The New Teddy Bear

Johnny didn't own a teddy bear. There were teddies in the house but they belonged to Johnny's older brother and sister.

When Johnny had been born, everyone agreed that new babies shouldn't be given teddy bears. "New babies suck and chew things — they are happier with rattles and building blocks."

"But he is such a sweet little thing," Johnny's sister, Mary, had said, looking into Johnny's cot. "Do you think we're being unkind not to give him a teddy?"

"We are doing the right thing," said Peter, Johnny's brother.

Peter was big enough to go to school and knew everything.

"We shall give Johnny a teddy when he is old enough to look after it properly," Peter said in a firm voice. "It wouldn't be fair to any teddy to give it to Johnny now. Teddy bears are usually good-tempered, but even the best of them don't like having their ears chewed or their feet sucked until they are wet and soggy."

Mary clutched at her ears. "I certainly would not like having my ears chewed," she shuddered. "I suppose having wet, soggy

feet would not be quite so bad, but I shouldn't really care for it."

"There you are, then," said Peter, smiling round at everyone. "We're doing the right thing. Johnny will be given a teddy when he is old enough to know how to treat a loyal friend."

Peter smiled at his own teddy, who was sitting at the window watching for Grandma to come visiting.

The bear said nothing and continued to stare along the road.

"And there's something else to remember," went on Peter. "All teddy bears are faithful friends, of course, but some are not as good-tempered as others. Some teddies can be difficult and short-tempered. Suppose Johnny were given a short-tempered bear! He wouldn't know how to talk to it to keep it in a good mood."

The bear in the window looked at Peter. "I am sure you would manage to tell him, though," thought the bear.

Peter was a good and clever boy, but he did like telling everyone else what to do.

Weeks, months and years went by, and the time came when everyone agreed that Johnny was old enough to own a teddy bear.

"I will buy Johnny a teddy bear for his birthday present from Grandpa and me," said Grandma.

So, about a week before his birthday, Grandma called for Johnny and took him to the toy shop. "You choose the teddy you like best," said Grandma, "Then I will take him home and wrap

him up ready for your birthday."

It was a big toy shop with many, many bears sitting in rows, all staring in front of them. There were bears in every colour — pink, blue, brown, gold and from green to white. Some had long fur, some had short. Some had fat faces, some were thinner, with longer noses, and looked as if they knew a thing or two about what went on in the world.

"What sort of bear would you like, Johnny?" asked Grandma. "There's plenty of time. Look at them all."

Johnny looked along the rows of furry faces.

"I should like a real bear-looking bear," he said. "I should like a brown bear with a proper nose, who looks as if he could take care of himself — and me as well," Johnny went on, not wishing to hurt the feelings of any of the bears who might be listening. "Those pretty pink bears and blue bears with the babyish faces are all very well for big children of ten or twelve who are almost grown-up, but little chaps like me need a tough teddy who can hold hands when we are listening to thrilling stories. You know the sort I mean — when the wolf is chasing Red Riding Hood or the spider comes down to sit beside Little Miss Muffet."

"Quite right," smiled Grandma. "You want a brown bear with a brave face and fierce, flashing dark eyes."

"Yes," agreed Johnny, but then he added quickly, "his eyes should not be too fierce. I want a bear who can be fierce to other people, when necessary, but always nice and friendly to me."

"Very well," agreed Grandma. "There must be a bear like that here somewhere. We must look until we find him."

Johnny and Grandma looked along the rows of bears. They picked out several tough-looking, smallish, brown bears. They all appeared brave and reliable and as if they would be loyal friends to a boy who treated them properly. Johnny stared and stared. Which was the bear for him?

Then as Johnny looked into each furry face, one after the other, it seemed to him that the second bear from the left gave him a little smile and a quick wink with one of his bright, black eyes.

"That is the bear for me, please," Johnny said to Grandma, pointing at the second bear from the left.

"What a good choice," said Grandma. "He looks a fine fellow!"

So the second bear from the left was bought and given to Johnny on his birthday. How proud Johnny was that at last he was old enough to own a teddy bear.

Teddy was proud that Johnny had chosen him from all the other bears in the big toy shop. "I noticed Johnny as soon as he came in through the shop door," Teddy would say to the other toys in later years, "I knew at once that he and I would suit each other. I gave him a smile and a wink, you know. That's what made him choose me. And of course," Teddy would add, "I was the handsomest bear in the shop."

That was something Johnny discovered about his teddy. He was faithful and brave, but just a little vain. Johnny and Teddy would have a lot of adventures together because of Teddy's high opinion of himself.

However, all that lay in the future. For the moment, on that happy birthday, Johnny and Teddy were pleased that they had found each other and were going to be friends for the rest of their lives.

The Shy Bear

The Shy Bear first came to live with the Brown family, when Susan Brown was aged seven and when Mathew Brown was aged four.

Teddy Two, the new bear was called, because there was already a teddy bear living in the house. This was Share Bear.

Share Bear was a beautiful yellow colour and wore a smart red coat. He was a very fine bear in every way, yet somehow ever since he had arrived in the Brown household, there had been trouble.

The trouble was not Share Bear's fault, it was the fault of the visitor who had brought him as a present. The visitor didn't know the family well. He thought Susan was an only child. He didn't know that Mathew had arrived about a year and a half

before his visit.

"Here is a lovely teddy bear I have brought as a present for Susan," smiled the visitor, when he arrived. Then he noticed Mathew and felt awkward because he had no present for him. "Oh dear — I mean, here is a teddy bear for both the children to share," he gasped, which is, of course, how Share Bear got his name.

Now sharing a teddy bear between two children is always a difficult thing. When one child wants to take the bear for a walk, the other wants to keep it at home. When one child is sick and wishes to cuddle teddy in bed, the other child needs teddy to sit at its side while watching television, in case anything scary happens.

Susan Brown and Mathew Brown and Share Bear did their best to keep everything friendly, but no one could deny that there were some difficult moments which led to a certain amount of jealousy and bad feeling.

Mrs Brown said several times that she thought she ought to

buy another teddy bear so that the children had a bear each. Mr Brown said that was nonsense. "The children have plenty of toys," he said. "Susan has a nice doll and there are other cuddly toys. If we buy a second bear, we shall be spoiling them."

Then, one happy Christmas, Grandpa gave Susan a nurse's outfit (which she loved) and to Mathew, Grandpa gave a teddy bear. This was the bear who was called Teddy Two at first and later came to be called Shy Bear.

Dolly looked down at the two bears from her place on the shelf by the window. "Perhaps we shall have some peace in the house now," she thought. "Let's hope there will be no more squabbles about who takes teddy where. This new teddy can always go with Mathew and Share Bear can be Susan's bear."

Unfortunately this did not happen.

Share Bear, as always, was bright and cheerful and ready to join in any fun. The new bear, Teddy Two, hung back and said nothing and didn't seem eager to do anything.

"I don't think that Teddy Two likes me," said Mathew.
"I want to keep my half share in Share Bear. I want Share Bear to come with me to play on the swings in the park,"

"But I want Share Bear to come with me next door to play

with my friend, Sandra," said Susan. "You can't have Share Bear this afternoon, Mathew. Share Bear must come with me."

Dolly looked down at Teddy Two.

"What's the matter with you?" she asked. "Why do you sit there saying nothing? You can hear how the children are quarrelling. I am sure Grandpa brought you here to stop all that. Wouldn't you like to go to the swings with Mathew?"

The new bear blushed and shuffled his feet and at last he managed to speak. "I'd love to go to the swings," he said, "but I don't wish to push myself forward. Share Bear was here before me. I feel that he should have first choice at everything."

"What nonsense!" gasped Dolly. "Share Bear will be quite happy to be Susan's bear. He has often told me that trying to please both the children was hard work. He will be glad if you take over his duties with Mathew."

Again Teddy Two looked down and blushed. "Well, I'm not one to push myself forward," he repeated. "I'll wait till Mathew asks me to go to the swings again, then I will see if he is really certain he wants me to go, and if Share Bear is absolutely sure

he doesn't want to go, and if Mrs Brown promises I shall not have to meet a lot of strangers while we are out, then I might go."

Dolly stared at Teddy Two.

"I see what is wrong now," she said. "You're shy!"

The new teddy blushed more than ever. "I know I am," he said.

Dolly frowned. "I thought you teddy bears were supposed to be trained how to behave," she said. "Why weren't you trained not to be shy?"

The new teddy bear dropped his eyes and shifted from one foot to the other. "I was trained," he said, "but I was bottom of the class. I only just scraped through my final exams."

For a moment he looked defiantly up at Dolly. "We can't all be clever," he said. "Everyone knew that I was not the best teddy bear in the world, but they said they would give me a chance. I must make good here with the Browns or I shall be taken back to Teddy Bear Land and have to go through my training all over again."

Teddy gave a little sob, "It was such hard work," he grunted, "and the exams were so difficult."

Dolly felt sorry for him. "I'll help you," she said. "When no one is watching and when Mathew is dozing off to sleep, I'll have a little chat with him. He will think he is dreaming. I'll say that you are shy. I will tell him that really you like him very much."

"Oh, I do. I DO!" said Teddy Two.

"And," went on Dolly, "I will tell Mathew that all you need is a little encouragement and you will become a wonderful friend."

That evening Dolly did as she had promised. The next day Mathew took another look at Teddy Two. He took him by the paw.

"Don't be shy," said Mathew. "Come to the swings with me and Mum this afternoon. Don't worry about Share Bear. He's looking forward to going shopping with Susan and Grandpa.

Don't worry about meeting new people. I will hold your paw and you need not feel nervous about anything."

Teddy Two was so grateful. He slipped his paw into Mathew's hand and they went out together and had a wonderful afternoon.

For weeks after that, Mathew took Teddy Two out and about and held his paw and patted his head if ever he started blushing or acting shyly. Everyone was happy. Mathew was happy because he felt grown-up and important helping Teddy Two. Teddy Two felt happy because he knew he was improving and starting to behave as a proper teddy should. Share Bear was happy because he no longer had to do the work of two bears, and Susan was happy because she had Share Bear all to herself. Dolly was happy because all the squabbling had stopped.

Teddy Two never had to go back to Teddy Bear Land to do his training over again. He never had to take another exam. Because of Mathew's kind help and understanding, Teddy Two got over his shyness and became one of the finest teddy bears that ever was.

"You know," said Dolly one day, "I think you should go back to Teddy Bear Land just for a quick day visit and take your final exam again. You have improved so much that this time I think you would be top of the class."

Teddy Two smiled, "Thank you for having so much confidence in me," he said, "but I don't think I will bother. I am so happy here with Mathew, I don't want to go away, not even for a single day."

And he never did.

The Mystery of Bigfoot Bear

Snowy Bear's fur was white. He was a polar teddy bear, quite used to cold weather and to looking after himself. Snowy, like all polar bears, was not afraid of anything or anybody.

When the time came for Snowy Bear to leave Teddy Bear Land, he climbed aboard the coach with the other young teddy bears and started to ride along the Forest Highway which led from Teddy Bear Land through miles and miles and MILES of forest until it came to other, even longer, roads which led to all the top shops in the world.

Snowy Bear shifted restlessly in his seat near the door of the coach. He glanced round at the other young teddies. "I don't know about the rest of you, but I feel like having a few adventures on my own before I settle down with a family," he said.

The other bears looked away and pretended not to hear. They had all decided that they wanted to become loyal friends to boys and girls as soon as possible. They could think of nothing nicer.

As it happened, Snowy was the only polar teddy on the coach. He tapped the driver on the shoulder. "You see that huge old redwood tree just ahead," he grunted. "Please stop the coach there and let me get out. In three years' time I will come back and wait by the same redwood. You can pick me up and take me on to the shops then, when I have seen a bit of the world."

The driver put on the brakes and slowed the coach to a halt.

"Suit yourself," he said. "See you in three years' time."

Coach drivers are like taxi drivers. Nothing much surprises them.

Snowy Bear climbed down the steep steps out of the coach and stood at the side of the road breathing the fresh air of freedom. The coach door snapped shut and the driver let in the clutch and started to drive away. Before the coach gathered speed, the driver rolled down his window and, poking out his head, called back to Snowy, "Keep a look out for Muncher Bear. He got out of the coach, just like you. About five years ago it was. Muncher Bear — that was the name. I'll always remember him because he was such a big chap. He looked like those grizzly bears and he never stopped eating — sandwiches, peanuts, cakes. We were clearing the coach of crumbs for weeks after he travelled with us. If you see him, give him my regards."

The coach driver's window shut again and the coach became smaller and smaller in the distance until it was gone from sight. Snowy Bear stepped off the road into the thick, dark forest. He headed north-west towards the mountains of northern California. He had never been happier.

Snowy spent several months learning to live on his own in the forest. He ate berries and tree bark, and fish from the rivers and lakes. He licked honey from the nests of the wild bees (which made them even wilder!) and he slept in caves or snuggled down amongst deep drifts of dead leaves.

One evening, when he was drinking water from a clear stream, he saw enormous footprints in the mud by the river bank. Snowy stared at them in amazement. He measured his own foot against them. The footprints in the mud were much, much larger. Snowy swallowed and looked carefully around. Being a polar teddy bear, he was not afraid of anything or anybody — but there was no harm in being careful.

He looked again at the footprints. They had four toes and claw marks at the end of the toes. They were like bear prints in a way. Snowy decided to follow them. Although he was enjoying life in the mountains, he hadn't spoken to anyone for weeks and the thought of a chat and a laugh with another bear was rather nice.

"I will go carefully and make sure I see him before he sees me," thought Snowy. "If he looks a rough, grumpy type, I can always slip away between the trees and no harm done."

Snowy followed the huge footprints away from the river and at once they became more difficult to track. Snowy had to look for scratch marks on the hard ground, and where the creature had snapped off branches as it pushed between the trees.

"He must be a huge fellow," Snowy was thinking, when he came to a clearing and saw a simply enormous teddy bear sitting at the mouth of a cave eating the berries from a bush, which he had pulled up as he walked through the forest. All around the cave were the remains of enormous meals. Snowy had not the slightest doubt. He had found Muncher Bear.

Snowy Bear coughed to warn Muncher that he was there. It never does to startle big bears, especially bears which are so very much bigger than you. Either leave them alone or be polite.

Snowy stepped forward and smiled.

"Mr Muncher Bear, I presume," he said, holding out a paw. "May I take the liberty of introducing myself? I am Snowy Bear from Teddy Bear Land. I got off the coach on the Forest Highway just as you did. And may I say how pleased I am to see you looking so well?"

Muncher Bear stopped eating and stared at Snowy for several seconds without speaking.

"Have they sent you to find me?" he asked, looking, if anything, a little nervous. "I won't go back, you know. I had

JAM
CREAM
PIZZA
HONEY
CHOCOLA

enough of being laughed at for eating so much. I like it here in this lonely forest where I can eat day in day out with no one to sneer at how big I am growing, or at my table manners."

He looked defiantly at Snowy. "I know I got very low marks in my table manners exam back in Teddy Bear Land, but how can anyone bother about table manners when they are feeling hungry all the time?"

"How indeed!" murmured Snowy Bear, trying not to notice how Muncher Bear wiped the berry juice from his mouth with the back of his paw, and then wiped his paw clean down the front of his furry chest.

Seeing that Muncher Bear was not fierce, but if anything shy, for the moment at least, Snowy Bear stepped forward into the clearing. "No one sent me and I have not come to take you back to Teddy Bear Land," he said. "I, too, am travelling round a little, and the driver of the coach I was on mentioned that I might see you. Now that I have found you, perhaps we could have a couple of days together talking about old times?"

Muncher Bear appeared to be doubtful, then nodded. "You are welcome to share my cave for a day or two," he said, "but only if you don't make remarks about how much I eat."

Suddenly he looked fierce and Snowy half stood up, ready to make a run for the shelter of the forest.

"You do know how to find your own food?" growled Muncher Bear anxiously. "You won't want to eat any of my food, will you?"

Snowy sat down again. "Of course not," he smiled soothingly. "I am good at finding my own food. You have no need to worry."

So Snowy Bear spent several days in the mountain cave with Muncher Teddy Bear and heard all about his adventures.

The first thing he learnt was that Muncher was no longer called Muncher. Now he was known as Bigfoot.

"Not that I mind what anyone calls me," sighed Bigfoot, as Snowy now called him, "so long as they leave me alone."

Then Snowy learnt that Bigfoot's trouble had started way back in Teddy Bear Land. Apparently Bigfoot was always hungry. He could not help it, that was the way he was. Naturally, as he was always hungry, he was always eating. People used to laugh at him and call him greedy. Then they started sneering at his table manners.

"Just because I always leant forward and took the food first, and because I took the biggest share, people were cross with me," said Bigfoot.

"Amazing!" muttered Snowy.

"You would think they could have understood that I was always so hungry I needed the food more than they did," said Bigfoot, with tears in his eyes.

"Some people are so selfish!" agreed Snowy.

Then Bigfoot went on to explain that he had made up his mind he would never be happy living with others and that he must find a lonely place and live by himself. He had left the coach on the Forest Highway and travelled far and wide over northern America. The more he ate the bigger he grew, and the bigger he grew the more he ate.

"Sometimes I was quite happy," smiled Bigfoot. "At first I saw only tribes of Indians. They called me Sasquatch and kept well away from me, which was fine. Then the miners started coming up into the mountains. I had a lovely home under some cyprus trees near a clear stream. I was happy there until a miner came and camped there too. I tell you, I was so cross I picked him up in his sleeping bag and carried him for miles and dumped him in a valley with a family of real bears I happened to know. He escaped after a while and told anyone who would listen that he had been kidnapped by apemen with big feet. That was when everyone started called me Bigfoot.

"I kept moving on after that," went on Bigfoot, "sometimes I was short of food. Once I went to a cabin where some humans were living and took some fish from a barrel. The fuss they made! They asked some miners to help them drive me away — all because I had taken a few fish. Well, perhaps it was more than a few — actually it might have been their whole supply for the winter. Still," Bigfoot looked at Snowy, "that was no reason to turn so bad-tempered, was it?"

"Any fair minded person should have understood that you needed the food more than they did," agreed Snowy. Even though he did not fear anything or anybody, Snowy thought it best to agree with a companion so much larger than he was.

"Then the miners started shooting at me," complained Bigfoot, "which I thought was quite uncalled for. I had not touched their fish after all, mostly because I didn't know where they had hidden them, I agree, but nevertheless I didn't touch them. I hid amongst the trees and, when night fell, I went to the miners' cabin and jumped on the roof and hammered at the door and really frightened them I can tell you." Bigfoot smiled at the happy memory. "After that I kept away from people as much as I could. I live in the high, lonely forest, eating as much as I like with no one to jeer at me. People do sometimes catch sight of me — or my footprints — and run about shouting and screaming 'BIGFOOT! HELP!' Then other folk come and search around, but the fuss always dies away. I tell you, Snowy, when you go back to catch that coach on the Forest Highway, you can tell the driver that I am happy and content."

Snowy smiled, "That is more than many can say," he murmured.

After a few days, Snowy went on his way and never saw Bigfoot Bear again. When finally he caught the coach at the redwood tree on the Forest Highway, he went on to be a loyal friend to a very nice boy. They often sat listening to the radio or watching television together. Sometimes Snowy would hear news reports of people seeing footprints of Bigfoot in America, or of explorers glimpsing something called a Yeti near a mountain called Everest, or of people in Australia seeing a strange creature called a Yowie, or other Australians out in the bush being jumped on by a Bunyip at a waterhole.

Snowy would smile and say to his owner, "I don't know about the Yeti, or the Yowie, or the Bunyip, but I do know for certain that Bigfoot is none other than old Muncher Bear from Teddy Bear Land."

HONEY

The Teddy Bear who Loved Trains

Once upon a time there was quite an ordinary sort of teddy bear, who lived with a boy named Michael. This bear was a medium size and a medium colour. He was never loud or pushy, but he was always there, ready for a chat or a cuddle whenever Michael needed him.

The only special thing about this teddy was that he did seem to like trains. Michael noticed that whenever he brought out the train set, Teddy's eyes did seem to sparkle. Michael was a kind, thoughtful boy. Whenever he played with trains, he sat Teddy so that the bear could watch all the fun.

When Michael was little, he had a wooden train which he

pulled along on a piece of string. When he grew older he was given a plastic train set with rails, which he could join together into different shaped tracks. There were bridges and stations and turntables, and a brightly coloured train which he pushed along by hand.

Michael loved his plastic train set. He spent hours joining the rails together in different ways and pushing the train to and fro. Always, before he started to play trains, Michael fetched Teddy and sat him where he could see everything that happened. Teddy's face used to shine with happiness.

Time went by and Michael grew older, not quite old enough to go to school, but old enough to go to the cinema if he went with a grown-up and the film was for children.

One evening Daddy came rushing home from work.

"Have you seen what film is showing at the cinema next week?" he asked in an excited voice. "It's The Great Toy Train Race!"

Daddy beamed at Michael.

"It's the perfect film for a boy like you," he said. "You love toy trains and so do I. I mean, I don't mind going to please you. Shall we go and see it together?"

Daddy looked at Mummy.

"You can come too if you want, but I don't think you're very interested in trains, are you?"

"No," smiled Mummy, "I think I might be more interested in an afternoon's rest and a quiet cup of tea."

Michael had noticed before that mothers had very strange ideas. They always liked sitting chatting to each other on the park bench, rather than sliding on the big slides. They always walked on the dry parts of the roads and car parks, instead of jumping in the puddles and making lovely splashes. Sometimes grown-ups were difficult to understand.

Michael smiled at Daddy.

"I should love to see The Great Toy Train Race," he beamed.

"We'll go on Saturday afternoon," said Daddy.

For the rest of the week the house was full of excited talk about the film; how there were ten different toy trains in it; how the toy railway lines went through jungles full of tigers and over rivers full of crocodiles; how trees blew over in front of the trains; and how the end of the race was so exciting that everyone who saw it cheered until they wore out their voices.

Michael was so happy. Then he saw Teddy, sitting, listening to all the eager talk. Teddy's face was full of longing. Michael knew at once that Teddy wanted to see the film.

Michael sat and thought. This was not going to be easy. Michael himself was growing older. Chatting to, and cuddling Teddy at home, was one thing. Being seen carrying a teddy bear out in the street might be thought babyish. Michael gritted his teeth. He would do it for the sake of pleasing Teddy.

However, there was Daddy to think about. Mummy was used to going out with children. Michael had two older sisters and for years Mummy had let them take dolls and push along toy dogs

and teddies to the shops.

Would Daddy want to bother with taking a teddy bear to the cinema?

Michael asked Daddy that evening.

Daddy groaned.

"I don't want to be seen carrying a teddy through the streets," he said.

"Oh, I'll carry him," replied Michael.

From where he was sitting by the window, Teddy looked hopeful.

"No!" said Daddy. "That would be even worse. You will get so interested in the film, you will forget about Teddy. You'll drop him and he'll get kicked away under the seats. We shall come home without him. Then at bedtime, you will remember him and be upset and I shall have to go back to the cinema. Oh what a fuss! No! No! Teddy must stay at home."

Teddy's ears drooped. He looked very disappointed. Michael felt guilty. How could he enjoy the film when Teddy was at home moping?

From being a lovely treat, the trip to the cinema was becoming a heartbreak.

Mummy noticed that Michael was looking glum and she knew why.

"We have two problems," she said. "Neither you nor Daddy want to be seen carrying a teddy through the streets, and Daddy is afraid that Teddy will be dropped. I know exactly what to do. Fortunately," went on Mummy, "it's wintertime and you will be wearing your coat. I will tie some string firmly round Teddy's waist. Then I will tie the string to a belt and fasten the belt round you, over one shoulder and under the other arm. In that way Teddy will be firmly fixed to the front of your chest. When your coat is done up he won't show and, when you undo your coat in the cinema, Teddy will have a good view of the film and he won't be dropped to the floor."

Michael was so pleased. Daddy agreed to take both Michael and Teddy to the cinema, so long as everything was done as Mummy had planned.

Teddy was thrilled. On the Saturday, Michael and Daddy and he went to see the film and had a wonderful time. The Great Toy Train Race was as exciting as everyone had said it was.

"How lucky I am," thought Teddy, "to have a kind, loyal owner like Michael and how lucky he is to have such understanding parents."

Belinda Bear to the Rescue

Jennifer was a good, neat, tidy girl. Her teddy bear, Belinda was a good, neat, tidy bear. Belinda Bear always wore clean, smart, fashionable clothes. She was a pink, washable bear and was always spotless. Belinda didn't mind going through the washing machine.

"Perhaps the spinning at the end does make me feel a little giddy," Belinda would remark to the other toys, "but one has to suffer to be beautiful. That's an old French saying, you know."

Belinda Bear once visited Paris. It was true that during the visit she had been in Jennifer's father's hand-luggage, because she was a present he was bringing home from a business trip but, nevertheless, she had managed to peep out through the zip at the top of the bag and had seen the elegant clothes in the shop windows and admired them very much.

"Paris is a very fashionable place. I know. I have been there,"

Belinda would say to the other toys. She felt it was her duty to dress as well as possible, in order to pass on some of the elegance she had seen in Paris to the other less well-travelled toys.

"Someone has to keep up standards, you know!" Belinda Bear would smile, patting her clean, fluffy fur and smoothing her skirt.

The other more comfy old toys, like Push-along Pony, who was far too big to go into the washing machine and who was rather dusty and worn, used to raise their eyebrows at Belinda Bear.

"If you had spent years being pushed round the garden helping the children of the family learn to walk, you would not look quite so fashionable," Push-along Pony neighed. "A few falls into the muddy flower beds and having your fur torn on rose bush thorns would soon spoil your neat appearance."

"I dare say," smiled Belinda Bear, "and I am sure the family treasures you for your unselfish service — in spite of your scruffy appearance. However, we all have our places in life. Yours is to be loved for being such a wonderful, if grubby, person."

Belinda Bear broke off to take a glance in the mirror.

"My place is to be admired and respected for my smart appearance. And of course," she hastened to add, "most of all my duty is to be a faithful friend to Jennifer."

No teddy bears, not even a fashionable one like Belinda, ever forgot that their first duty was to be loyal to their owners.

In truth, Belinda Bear and Jennifer suited each other very well. Jennifer always tried to look her best and she was pleased to have a teddy bear who did the same. Jennifer and her mummy were good at needlework and knitting. Many were the happy hours they spent making clothes and dressing up.

Then, one day, the Great Adventure happened.

Jennifer had a brother several years older than herself. He was so old he knew how to drive a car! His name was Jason. Jason was big and noisy. He was always slamming in and out of the house with his friends, leaving muddy footprints, dropping magazines and playing loud music.

"A very nice young man I am sure, deep-down," Belinda Bear would think, "but thank goodness I was given to Jennifer and not to Jason. Jennifer suits me much better." (It's remarkable how

teddy bears always seem to go to the boy or girl who suits them best, but everything about teddy bears usually works out well).

That weekend Jason had arranged to go on a car rally with his friend, Brian. Car rallies are events where people have to drive their cars to certain places at certain times. They have to read maps and find their way along surprise routes. Sometimes they have to arrive with certain special things which they have bought along the way. They mustn't travel too fast and they mustn't travel too slowly. Sometimes their cars can win prizes for being clean and polished. At the end of the rally, those who have reached the right place at the right time have a nice lunch together and laugh and talk about their adventures.

Jason and Brian thought car rallies were great fun.

Jason had arranged to borrow his mother's car for the rally and he had cleaned and polished it until it shone. Brian's father had given him a lift to Jason's house and the two boys were about to leave for the rally, when Brian gasped in horror.

"I've forgotten our mascot!" he wailed. "Tubby Bear! My faithful old teddy! I've left him at home on the hall table! How can we go on the rally without a mascot? We shall have nothing but bad luck. In any case it's a Teddy Bear Car Rally. No one can take part without a teddy bear mascot inside the car!"

The two young men were in despair. If they drove to Brian's home for Tubby Bear they would be late for the start of the rally.

Mummy and Jennifer and Belinda Bear had been standing in the porchway waiting to wave goodbye to the two young men. Jennifer looked at Belinda and Belinda looked at Jennifer. They both knew what they had to do.

Belinda Bear thought of all the swaying and bumping round corners and the music which Jason always had blaring from the speakers in the car. Jennifer looked at Belinda's pretty dress, which she had spent hours sewing and did not wish to see creased in the heat of a hot car, but this was no time to be selfish.

"Will you go?" Jennifer whispered into Belinda's ear.

Belinda gritted her teeth and gave a brave nod.

Jennifer held Belinda Bear out to Jason.

"You may take Belinda as your mascot, if you wish," she said. "I am sure she will try her best to bring you luck and she is a bear anyone can be proud of."

Jason knew how much Jennifer loved Belinda.

"Will you really part with her for a day?" he asked. "Are you sure you can manage without her?"

Jennifer nodded.

"I shall miss her very much," she said, "but we must help each other. That's what families are for."

"Thank you Jennifer, you're wonderful!" beamed Jason. He put Belinda on the back shelf of the car where she could look out of the window and he patted her on the head.

"Bring us luck, old girl!" he grinned.

Belinda shuddered.

Old girl indeed! What a way to speak to a well-dressed young lady bear, who had once visited Paris!

As the car drove away up the road, Belinda watched the small figure of Jennifer for as long as she could.

"Jennifer is a marvellous sister to lend her teddy for almost a whole day," thought Belinda.

Standing by the garden gate, Jennifer watched Belinda's pink face growing smaller and smaller as the car raced further and further away.

"That rally is going to be a rough ride for an elegant bear like Belinda," she thought, "but I'm sure I can rely on her to do her duty wonderfully. Teddy bears are so dependable."

Jason and Brian drove to the starting point. They jumped out and waved papers and tickets, and talked excitedly to official-looking people wearing arm bands and to other young men.

"Show us your teddy bear. No one can take part without a teddy," Belinda heard a voice say.

At once the door of the car was wrenched open and Jason grabbed Belinda by the arm, waved her round his head and plomped her down — THUMP! — on a table.

"Here is the smartest teddy bear in the world!" he grinned. "She's going to bring us wonderful luck and Brian and I are going to win all the prizes — best turned-out car, best time-keepers, the lot."

Some of the other young men laughed and one of them even tweaked Belinda's ear.

"This certainly is an improvement on old Tubby Bear," he said, "but she'll have to struggle till she bursts at the seams to bring you two enough luck to win any prizes with your dull, little car. My snappy sports car is sure to win everything."

Then the young man took a closer look at Belinda.

"She's unusually smart," he agreed. "You probably stand a chance of winning the prize for the best-dressed teddy bear. Anyway, we shall find out at the end of the day."

A brisk wind blew across the road, mussing up Belinda's fluffy pink fur. Jason snatched her up again and sat her back in the car. After a few minutes Brian and Jason climbed into the front seats and started reading from a sheet of instructions and looking at a map, and at their watches, and arguing.

"Under the railway bridge and past the Blue Cow Cafe is the best way to the ruined castle," said Jason.

"No! Round by the school and along by the river is quicker," snapped Brian. "And that road leads near to the shops. We've got to be at the ruined castle with a bag of twelve apples by eleven o'clock, and then drive on to the Brown Bull Farm by twelve

o'clock with a bag of six biscuits, and then on to the Apple Pie Restaurant by one o'clock with two bars of chocolate as it says in these instructions. Not to mention driving between the ruined castle and the Brown Bull Farm at thirty kilometres an hour, and between the Brown Bull Farm and the Apple Pie Restaurant at fifty kilometres an hour, and being allowed five minutes to clean the car in the car park of the Apple Pie Restaurant. So first, we must drive past the shops so that we can buy the eleven apples and the twelve biscuits and the one bar of chocolate."

"No!" interrupted Jason, snatching the piece of paper and reading it again. "You've got that wrong. We've got to buy twelve apples not eleven, and we need a bag of six biscuits, not twelve, and I'm sure you said two bars of chocolate."

Brian started going red in the face and peered again at the piece of paper, which was already creased and grubby from being crumpled in the boys' hands.

"I'm sure it was eleven apples by twelve o'clock at the ruined castle and twelve biscuits by six o'clock at the Brown Bull Farm and one chocolate bar by two o'clock at the Apple Pie Restaurant," he wailed. "No! That can't be right. Let me read it all again, if I can — this paper is in such a mess!

Then one of the officials wearing an arm band waved a flag at the car and Jason had to drive off. The rally had started.

Belinda patted her pink fur back into place.

"I can see these young men need all the help I can give them" she thought, "and even then I doubt if they will win anything. If they can't remember a simple thing like being at the ruined castle with a bag of twelve apples by eleven o'clock, driving to Brown Bull Farm by twelve o'clock with a bag of six biscuits and then on to the Apple Pie Restaurant by one o'clock with two bars of chocolate; drive between the Brown Bull Farm at thirty kilometres an hour; drive between the Brown Bull Farm and the Apple Pie Restaurant at fifty kilometres an hour and finally spend five minutes cleaning the car in the car park of the Apple Pie Restaurant, there is little hope for them. However," she smoothed her skirt, "I do feel we stand a good chance of winning the prize for the best-dressed teddy bear."

Now, in the ordinary way of things, Jason and Brian were two sensible and bright young fellows, but taking part in a rally was thrilling and important. That was why they were in such a muddle. Their hands were hot and sticky and their brains were working faster than usual and giving all the wrong answers.

No doubt most children could remember all those instructions as easily as Belinda did. Jason and Brian, however, could not.

"Open the car windows to cool us down," gasped Brian.

Down rolled the windows and in blew the wind. The sheet of instructions and map blew up over Jason's face and on to the back shelf where Belinda grabbed them and sat on them before they could be sucked out into the road. Jason slammed on the brakes and BUMP! Belinda and the instructions and the map thumped down on to the car floor.

"So far, so bad!" gasped Belinda. "A fine mascot I'm turning out to be. Obviously I must try much harder than this."

Brian leaned over the front seat, grabbed up Belinda, threw her back on to the shelf, and took the sheet of instructions and the map into the front of the car.

"Oh no!" he groaned. "The instructions are torn in the place where the numbers are written. I can't read any of them now."

Jason glanced over his shoulder as he re-started the car.

"Sorry about all this, Belinda," he called, "but we must get on with the rally." He slammed the car into gear and it leapt forward.

Belinda gripped the edge of the shelf and managed to smile.

"Thank you for your kind apology, which I accept," she

murmured politely, not reproaching Jason because she had dust on her fur and her dress was creased.

For a few moments Belinda was upset. There was no chance now of winning the prize for being the best dressed teddy bear. Then she shook herself and sat up straight.

"It was wrong of me ever to think of a prize for myself," she said. "Teddy bears must always put their owners first and, as Jennifer has lent me to Jason, I must think of nothing but helping Jason to do well in the rally and win one of the prizes."

Now teddy bears are quite good at counting. In Teddy Bear Land they are all trained to count up to one hundred, which is very clever. Of course some bears are better than others, and some do forget a lot of their training as the years go by, but fortunately, Belinda Bear had a good memory. Merely from hearing Brian read out the rally instructions once, she could remember them. Belinda sat on the back shelf of the car thinking over and over to herself: "Be at the ruined castle with a bag of twelve apples by eleven o'clock. Be at the Brown Bull Farm by twelve o'clock with a bag of six biscuits. Be at the car park of the Apple Pie Restaurant by one o'clock with two bars of chocolate. Drive between the ruined castle and the Brown Bull Farm at thirty kilometres an hour. Drive between the Brown Bull Farm and the Apple Pie Restaurant at fifty kilometres an hour. In the car park of the Apple Pie Restaurant, clean the car for five minutes."

Jason swerved into a lay-by near some shops.

"Brian," he gasped, "rush into that supermarket and buy eleven apples and twelve biscuits and one bar of chocolate, while I stay here with the engine running so that we can hurry on with the rally."

Brian hesitated.

"Are you sure it wasn't one apple, twelve biscuits and eleven bars of chocolate?" he asked anxiously.

Belinda thought as hard as she had ever thought in her life.

"Twelve apples, six biscuits and two bars of chocolate," she thought over and over again.

As Brian hurried across to the shops, the words twelve apples, six biscuits and two bars of chocolate came dancing into his head. He bought the correct number of everything and leapt back into the car. Off they roared with Belinda swinging about on the back shelf. The stitches of the sleeve of her dress tore apart, but she didn't care. All she thought of was helping Jason.

"At least we've done the shopping," puffed Jason, "although I'm not at all sure you've bought the right number of things. Are you sure it shouldn't have been thirty apples and fifty biscuits and five bars of chocolate?"

"No! No!" shouted Brian. "Now you are getting muddled up with how fast we are supposed to drive and how many minutes we'll have to clean the car at the end of the journey."

Belinda swivelled round and looked out at the road. She was beginning to feel a tiny bit car sick, but she was not going to admit it, not even to herself.

"The shopping has been done correctly," she thought. "Now I must make them drive at the right speed."

Jason suddenly slammed on the brakes. They had reached the open space next to the ruined castle. He rolled down the window and handed the bag of apples to one of the rally officials who was standing waiting.

"That's right, twelve apples!" smiled the man. "You would never believe how many people get that wrong."

"Amazing!" said Brian. "Fancy making a mistake like that."

The official patted the bonnet of the car. "You're on time and doing well," he smiled. "Continue on the rally."

Jason started the engine and drove the car towards Brown Bull Farm. He and Brian looked round to find the instructions to have one more attempt at reading them. Brian picked a few muddy shreds of paper from beneath his feet.

"The instructions must have stuck to my shoes as I got out to do the shopping," he groaned. "Now they are so torn and muddy there's no hope of reading them at all."

"We shall have to do our best to remember," said Jason putting his foot down on the car accelerator. "I think it was fifty kilometres an hour between here and the Brown Bull Farm."

"No! No!" said Brian. "It was five kilometres an hour here and thirty kilometres an hour between the Brown Bull Farm and the Apple Pie Restaurant."

Belinda Bear sat on the back shelf thinking over and over again, "Thirty kilometres an hour between the ruined castle and Brown Bull Farm, fifty kilometres an hour between Brown Bull Farm and Apple Pie Restaurant, and five minutes in the Apple Pie Restaurant car park for cleaning the car."

The wonderful little bear thought of the instructions with so much strength that at last they popped across into the heads of Jason and Brian. The two young men drove the rally at exactly the correct speeds and arrived at Brown Bull Farm and the

Apple Pie Restaurant at the proper times and of course, they handed in the right numbers of biscuits and chocolate bars. They won the prizes for the best time-keeping and the smartest car. Belinda Bear was so happy for them that she didn't give a thought to missing the prize for the best-dressed teddy bear.

After lunch, Jason and Brian drove home with Belinda Bear squashed between them in the front of the car. Gravy and ice cream were splashed over her fur from where she had sat on the table joining in the fun at lunch time. The sleeve of her dress was hanging by a thread and her skirt was a mass of creases. How happy they all were!

"We won! We won!" called Jason and Brian running into the house, slamming the doors, leaving muddy footprints and waving Belinda round their heads.

Jason handed Belinda back to Jennifer. "She was a wonderful mascot," he laughed. "We could never have managed without her. She brought us the best luck in the world."

Then he noticed exactly how scruffy Belinda was looking.

"Oh dear! I am sorry!" he said. "Will she wash clean?"

"Yes," smiled Mum. "Belinda Bear never minds going through the washing machine and she always comes up looking like new."

"Oh good!" said Jason with a sigh of relief. "And tomorrow I will take Jennifer to the shops and buy a new dress for Belinda, and some sweets for Jennifer to thank her for lending me her dear bear."

Jennifer smiled and gave Belinda a hug.

"You can tell me all about what happened when we go to bed," she smiled, "and thank you for being such a wonderful bear."

While the family were having supper, Belinda Bear sat resting with the other toys. Push-along Pony looked at her in amazement.

"I never expected to see you looking scruffy," he neighed. "You look worse than I do."

"I'm afraid I do," Belinda agreed, "but we teddy bears have to do our duty, and much as I like to look smart, I had to forget about elegance today and put my thoughts towards being a good car mascot. Never mind! Tomorrow I shall have a good whizz round in the washing machine. I shall choose a marvellous new dress and I shall look as wonderful as ever."

Push-along Pony looked at Belinda in admiration.

"I always thought you were too interested in your appearance to do your duty properly as a loyal teddy bear," he said, "now I see I was wrong. Your heart is in the right place after all."

The Journey to Father Christmas Land

The land round about the North Pole is cold and covered with snow and ice for most of the year. There are wide stretches of sea which are frozen over and there are lots of islands, some large and some small. On one of these islands, according to Snowy Bear, lives Father Christmas. In the winter months this island is snow-covered, but for a few brief weeks in the summer the warm sunshine melts away part of the snow and beautiful flowers grow in the clearings and pathways between the trees.

When Father Christmas sets out on his Christmas journey, he travels by sledge pulled by flying reindeer, but for the remainder of the year he walks about on his island like everyone else.

The elves and fairies and teddy bears trot to and fro between the work-huts, pulling sledges loaded with toys. They also make the long dangerous journey to and from Teddy Bear Land. That journey is made partly by canoe across the sea, when the water melts in the summer-time, and partly by sledges pulled by reindeer. These are young reindeer being trained for the Christmas journeys, but who are not yet sensible and steady enough for the flights through the skies. In any case, flying, which is a magical thing, is only possible at Christmas.

The fairies and elves also travel to and from Fairyland, but Snowy Bear never discovered how that was done. Any fairies he asked about their journey muttered something like 'over the rainbow' and quickly changed the subject.

"People are entitled to keep their secrets," Snowy would say, "so I didn't ask any more."

Snowy Teddy Bear first went to Father Christmas Land by accident. It was springtime and he was exploring the dense woodland north of Teddy Bear Land, but not as far north as where Father Christmas lives. There are no roads in that wilderness and no people. The few track-ways are made by wild animals, some of whom can be fierce and unfriendly. There are wolves, and Arctic foxes with white fur, who can sneak up on you unseen and be very snappy. There are big, grizzly bears who have never been to Teddy Bear Land and have not been taught the proper way to behave. They never say 'please' or 'thank you', and Snowy Bear says that grizzlies will biff any stranger with their big paws before they have even said 'How do you do?'

If you ever ask Snowy Bear about the real, wild polar bears who live in the very far north, he doesn't say much.

"I don't like to hear bears speaking ill of their own families," he will growl, "I will say only this. I am sure those wild polar bears are fine fellows at heart, but they need understanding. You have to see things from their point of view. Unfortunately, before you know them well enough to see their point of view, they have usually eaten you! My advice to anyone who ever sees a real, wild polar bear is to run fast in the opposite direction. Of course, polar teddy bears are quite different. They are as brave and fearless as real polar bears, but they are lovable with it."

Anyway, this springtime, Snowy Bear was walking through the forest when, to his surprise, he came across a wider track than usual. There were the marks of reindeer hooves and sleigh runners in the melting, muddy snow.

"Goodness!" gasped Snowy. "This must be the track which leads from Teddy Bear Land to Father Christmas Land."

Snowy had left Teddy Bear Land two years previously and was doing some exploring before he settled down with a nice human family. He knew that one day he would go to a toy shop and be bought for a boy or girl. He also knew that some bears

chose to go directly to Father Christmas Land to be delivered by Father Christmas with the Christmas presents. He had heard that the journey to Father Christmas Land was rough, and could be dangerous.

"Everything is fine when things are going fine," a teddy had said to him, "but if things go wrong, you are in trouble."

"It hardly takes a mastermind to know that," Snowy had thought, but he had always remembered what the other teddy had said.

Now Snowy Bear sat by the track and waited. He felt in the mood to see some teddies fresh from Teddy Bear Land and to hear the latest gossip.

An hour or so had passed when, far in the distance, came the sound of reindeer snorting. There was the sharp sound of hooves striking stones and the squelchy sound as those same hooves splashed in and out of the mud. There was the rasping noise of sleigh runners sliding over the ground. The sounds grew louder, and round a curve in the track, came a large sledge pulled by two young reindeer and containing about twenty teddy bears. They were well wrapped up in blankets and there were hampers of food on the sledge and baskets, which Snowy later learnt contained presents for Father Christmas and Mrs Christmas.

Snowy stood up and smiled and waved, thinking that the sledge would stop. To his surprise, the teddies glanced at him in dismay, shook the reins, and shouted to the reindeer to go faster. Snowy ran along in the track of the sledge.

"Stop!" he called. "It's me — Snowy. I come from Teddy Bear Land, too. I only want to chat. Stop! Stop!"

The sledge continued to go forward, but it did slow down. Some of the teddies peered at Snowy over the back rail. He heard

them talking among themselves. Some were saying they must not stop. Stopping was forbidden because it was dangerous. Others were saying that they thought they did remember Snowy and there could be no harm in having a chat with him. Yet more were objecting that Snowy was too dirty and shaggy to be a teddy bear and that he must be one of those wild polar bears who had to be avoided at all costs.

The sledge never did stop, but it slowed down enough for Snowy to run at its side. The leader of the group, a very dashing and unusual lavender-coloured bear shouted, "I believe you are Snowy Bear. I remember you, even though you look so rough. I cannot stop. It is forbidden because of dangers from wolves and so on, but if you like to jump aboard, you are welcome to come with us to Father Christmas Land."

Snowy made up his mind at once. No one could miss a chance to meet Father Christmas. He leapt aboard the sledge and at once Lavender Teddy shouted at the reindeer to go fast again.

"Exploring through these forests may be fine for you fearless polar teddies," said Lavender Teddy. "The wild creatures are afraid of you in case you turn out to be as nasty-tempered and strong as those wild polar bears, but for we other teddies this part of the forest is a dangerous place and we must keep on the move."

Snowy borrowed a towel to wipe the mud from his fur, then he settled down amongst the other bears and heard all the latest news, and ate some of the delicious egg sandwiches they had brought with them.

"This journey is fine when things are going fine, but if things go wrong then we are in trouble," said one of the bears, glancing round nervously.

"So I have been told," said Snowy.

In fact the journey was fine. The sledge rolled along the track in the spring sunshine, never hitting a rock or a tree root. The reindeer did not get tangled in their reins, nor take fright and break free and bolt amongst the trees. If any wolves or grizzlies or wild polar bears did stare out from the dark shadows of the forest, they decided that the sledge was travelling too fast to be

Snowy and his friends walking up the track to Father Christmas' home.

One of the elves is busy decorating the trees.

worth chasing. The sledge ran on for mile after mile and hour after hour. At last it topped a rise that looked down to the sea. There, at the water's edge, floating up and down amongst lumps of melting sea ice, were several large canoes sent by Father Christmas.

On the beach were two large wooden huts. One was a stable for the reindeer. One was a home for the elves who looked after the canoes.

"You made good time," called out one of the elves. "Jump aboard the canoes and we will paddle you across to the island and take you up to Father Christmas' house in time for supper." He looked at their anxious faces, for although everything on the journey had been fine, in their hearts all the bears, except Snowy, had been worried in case something had gone wrong and they had found themselves in trouble.

"Once you are on our island and in Father Christmas Land, you will be quite safe," smiled the elf. "There are no wild animals on our island. Anyone can walk anywhere without a care in the

world."

The teddies all smiled and hurried into the canoes and set off across the green, cold water. Once again the journey was safe. Before even the teddy with the weakest stomach could think about being seasick, they had landed on Father Christmas' island and walked up the flower-filled tracks to the clearing where Father Christmas lived. His home was wooden, built of trees felled when the clearing was made. It was large and comfortable with several floors and many rooms all with fireplaces and blazing log fires. There were cosy sitting rooms and comfortable bedrooms. There were kitchens where fairies and elves helped Mrs Christmas to cook enormous old-fashioned meals. There were dining rooms where everyone sat together at long tables and ate and chatted when the day's work was over.

Eating between meals was allowed, too.

Snowy says that a bear called Fireside Bear visited Father Christmas for two weeks every summer. He was a jolly fellow who was always toasting crumpets at one of the fireplaces. He

spread the crumpets with butter and ate them with anyone who would sit and join him. He always volunteered to bring in logs when they were needed or to clear out the ashes from the fireplaces. He never minded how much work he did.

"Being in a house with fireplaces is such a pleasure," he would beam. "When I go back to my human family, I live in a house with central heating. That's no fun. I don't mind how much I work I do here, with Father Christmas, so long as I can enjoy being by a fireside."

Of course, on his first visit, Snowy was eager to see what Father Christmas really looked like. It was summer-time and Snowy did wonder if the great man would be wearing his red furry outfit or if it would be too hot. Snowy was not disappointed. A little before supper-time, Father Christmas came stamping in from some of the work-huts where he had been watching over the packing of some farmyard sets.

"Remember to put in the little piglets with the mother pig and the fences for the pig sty," he had reminded an elf, who had become rather careless. "We cannot have any child being disappointed, can we?"

Snowy stared at Father Christmas as he came in through the door. He was tall and plump and jolly with long white hair and whiskers, and he wore a red hat and jacket and trousers. His suit was edged with fur and he wore big leather boots. He was exactly as everyone imagined him to be. This outfit he was wearing was of thin material for the summer and it was a little worn here and there because it was a working outfit, but this was Father Christmas, without a doubt.

Father Christmas saw Snowy staring at him.

"Yes," he smiled. "I wear this sort of outfit all the time. People expect it, and Father Christmas must never disappoint anyone. Mrs Christmas makes me two new suits a year, one for summer and one warm one to wear new each Christmas. I have to look smart for my Christmas journeys, you know."

He looked around.

"I suppose you arrived with the new batch of teddy bears. I'm glad you travelled here safely. That journey is fine when things are going fine, but if things go wrong, you are in trouble."

"So everyone says," replied Snowy.

For the next week or two Snowy spent a happy time in the land of Father Christmas. He learnt that, apart from two or three weeks' holiday, the whole year was spent in making and packing toys, training and looking after reindeer, building and mending sledges, keeping everything clean and tidy, and checking the workers in and out from Fairyland and the teddy bears in from Teddy Bear Land. The busiest time of the year was December, when Father Christmas' biggest sledge had to be loaded, and the strongest, trustiest reindeer needed to be fed with the finest oats and harnessed for their long journeys through the skies.

In some countries the children's toys were delivered at the beginning of December. In some countries they had to arrive on Christmas Eve. In other places New Year's Day was the correct delivery time. In some countries Father Christmas was called Father Christmas. In others he was known as Santa Claus, and in others he was Saint Nicholas. It seemed complicated, but Father Christmas understood it all and always made the correct deliveries.

When January came, Father Christmas was exhausted and overweight from eating all those mince pies and slices of cake which had been left out for him by the children.

"Never mind, I love every minute and every mouthful," he would smile, as he took a rest before starting the preparations for next Christmas.

A lot of people ask Snowy Bear if he found out whether Father Christmas sleeps with his whiskers over or under the sheets, and Snowy always says he thinks it depends on the

weather. In the winter he sleeps with them tucked down under the blankets to be warm, but in the summer he has them out on top of the sheets to be cool. That is what the elves who took Father Christmas his early morning tea said, and they should know.

After Snowy had spent several happy weeks with Father Christmas — doing his share of the work of course — he said he would like to continue his wanderings.

"I don't think that even a fearless teddy polar bear like you should explore in this far northern forest alone," said Father Christmas. "I am sending a sledge to Teddy Bear Land tomorrow to bring back another group of bears who will join me this summer. They only travel up in the summer, you know, the trail is blocked completely in the winter. You travel on that sledge with the driver and drop off somewhere down in Canada. Why don't you go to see my friend, Teddy Bear of the Mounties? He is a fine fellow and has led an adventurous life. You should persuade him to tell you about it."

Snowy thanked Father Christmas and agreed to take his advice.

The next day Father Christmas came on the sea crossing to the mainland to wave goodbye to Snowy.

"Good luck on the journey," he said, patting the younger reindeer and shaking hands with the driver and Snowy. "This journey is fine when things are going fine, but if things go wrong, you are in trouble."

Snowy always tried to be polite, but he could not hide a bored yawn, at hearing this remark yet again.

"You may yawn," said Father Christmas, "but once things did go wrong. It was when a group of teddies decided to go as presents to a country called Greece. One of them had given himself a Greek name. Xenophon it was. Who could forget a name like that? The troubles those bears went through! Next time you visit I will tell you the whole story."

"Thank you, I always love a good adventure story," smiled Snowy and he went on his journey down to Canada, feeling satisfied that at last he knew what Father Christmas was like.

You may be interested to know that Snowy did meet Teddy Bear of the Mounties, and he did go back to hear the story of Xenophon the Greek teddy bear. Anyone who searches around in this book may be lucky enough to find the stories that Snowy heard.

Teddy Bear of the Mounties

One day a fine, brave teddy bear was bought as a friend for a boy named Darren. Darren lived in Canada and he was proud of his great-grandfather who had been a member of the Royal North West Mounted Police, or Mounties, as they were called for short. Great-grandpa had been a Mountie when the land was wild and dangerous, and there were many tales told in the family about his adventures.

"I wish someone in the family was a Mountie now," said Darren.

"I agree," said his dad, "but things haven't worked out that way. I was good at sums when I was at school, so I had to become an accountant and Uncle Andy is good at writing, so he works for

a newspaper."

Seeing that Darren was disappointed, Dad said, "I know, let us make Teddy into a Mountie. I am sure that he is brave and loyal and everything that a good Mountie should be."

Darren thought this a great idea, and Teddy was pleased, too. Mum found some old photographs of Mounties and made Teddy a uniform as near as she could to the ones worn in those days of long ago. When Teddy was properly dressed, he and Darren were taken to visit Grandpa, who was the son of Great-grandpa Mountie. Grandpa knew everything worth knowing.

"Teddy looks smart," said Grandpa, "but he will not be a proper Mountie until he is sworn in."

Grandpa held up Teddy's paw.

"Do you promise to be brave and faithful and to do your duty?" he asked.

"I'm sure he does," said Darren. "You do, don't you, Teddy?"

Teddy nodded and from that day onwards he was Teddy Bear of the Mounties.

Teddy and Darren spent the rest of the afternoon with Grandpa, learning how a Mountie should behave.

"I'll tell you what Great-grandpa Mountie did," said Grandpa, "then if anything similar happens to you, you will know what is expected of you."

Grandpa explained that in Great-grandpa Mountie's days very few people had been living across the miles and miles of Canada. There were no cars, no aeroplanes and no nice wide roads. The few people who did venture out into the wilderness could get lost, or fall ill, or run short of food, and there was no one to help them. And, as Grandpa explained, there were some naughty people who did bad things and, in those days,they could escape into the wild country and never be caught. The Mounties were formed to put all that right. Mounties had to know how to ride horses, how to drive sledges pulled by husky dogs. They had to know how to find their way north, south, east or west, over mountains and across rivers. They had to know how to care for sick people, and how to hunt for food when supplies ran short.

Teddy Bear tugged at Darren's sleeve looking a little worried.

"I don't think I can learn how to do all that in one afternoon," he whispered.

Darren looked at Grandpa.

"Could we visit again tomorrow?" he asked. "I think Teddy needs two afternoons to finish his training properly."

"Visit as often as you like," beamed Grandpa.

So Teddy and Darren learnt that at first Great-grandpa Mountie had gone on patrol through the lonely lands where trappers trapped for fur, and where Indians hunted for food. No one knew the trails better than the Mounties did. Once, Great-grandpa found a trapper who had hurt his leg and couldn't walk or ride his horse. Great-grandpa bound up the leg, hoisted the trapper on to his horse, and led them back through blizzards and packs of howling, hungry wolves to safety.

Teddy Bear felt worried again. He knew that he would be brave and fight off the howling, hungry wolves, but he wasn't sure about finding his way. He was still having trouble with remembering which door led to Darren's bedroom on the home landing. Was it turn right at the top of the stairs and take the

second door on the left, or was it turn left at the top of the stairs and take the first door on the right?

Fortunately, Teddy heard Grandpa say that new Mounties always went out with older Mounties, until they had learnt all they needed to know. After that, Teddy Bear of the Mounties felt better.

Next, Grandpa explained that, in the 1890s, gold had been found in a place called the Klondike. That had led to a lot of trouble. Hundreds of people had rushed in, hoping to become rich. Most people had been polite, but there were some who caused trouble. One day, when he was on patrol, Great-grandpa Mountie met a gold miner who was very upset. This miner had worked hard for months and months and, as he was about to leave for home, a bandit had robbed him of his bag of gold.

"He was big and mean with curly hair and a bushy red beard," the miner had told Great-grandpa Mountie. "He had one brown eye and one blue, and a snake tattooed on his right arm."

"I'll find him for you and bring back your gold, no matter how long it takes," Great-grandpa Mountie had promised.

Great-grandpa Mountie kept his word. Over mountains and across rivers he went, through snow and through flood. He ran short of food, but always he trekked on to the next settlement. Everywhere he went he asked for news of the big, mean man with curly hair, a bushy red beard, one brown eye, one blue eye and a snake tattooed on his right arm.

At first Great-grandpa was told the man was three days ahead of him . . . then two days ahead of him . . . then one day ahead of him . . . then half a day ahead of him . . . then Great-grandpa Mountie caught him.

"Why didn't you tire of chasing me?" asked the man. "Why didn't you give up? Why do you care about that stupid miner?"

"The Mounties never tire of following the trail," said Great-grandpa. "They never give up, and they always care about citizens who have been wronged. The Mounties always get their man."

Then Great-grandpa Mountie took the gold back to the miner, who was pleased and grateful. The bandit with the curly hair and bushy red beard and one brown eye and one blue eye and a snake tattooed on his right arm, promised never to steal

again — at least not when the Mounties were looking.

Everyone got to know that the Mounties always went to help people in trouble, even in the furthest wilderness, and that they always chased bandits, however far they ran. People all across Canada slept peacefully in their beds because they knew the Mounties always got their man.

Teddy Bear of the Mounties gulped. "While I wear this uniform, I must try to behave so that the old Mounties would be proud of me," he thought.

Several months went by and Teddy Bear of the Mounties was not called upon to do anything more dangerous than keep clean and tidy, which Darren and Mum helped him with anyway. One day, a group of aunties and young cousins came visiting and brought their toys with them. Everyone had a great time, playing and chatting, and, during lunch, while Darren and his guests were eating, Teddy Bear of the Mounties and all the toys were left in the games-room. It had been a tiring morning and, to tell the truth, Teddy dozed off for a few minutes. He was woken by the sobs of Toy Tabby Kitten.

"I spent all morning collecting toy building bricks," said Tabby, "but as I was about to build them into a tall tower, a bad, mean, toy hippo took them and ran away with them."

Teddy looked around the room. Hippos were fashionable toys that year and several of them had come visiting.

"Did it have curly hair and a bushy red beard and one brown eye and one blue eye and a tattoo of a snake on its arm?" he asked, hoping that this bandit would be like the bandit chased by Great-grandpa Mountie. Bandits with curly hair and bushy red beards and one brown eye and one blue eye and a tattoo on their arm, were easy to follow because people noticed them.

"No," replied Herbie Hamster, "he was a plain, brown, fluffy hippo like all the others."

Teddy sighed. "Nothing is ever easy when it's your turn to do it," he said.

So Teddy of the Mounties started the long task of going to one plain, brown, fluffy hippo after another, asking if he had taken the building bricks from little Tabby Kitten. Teddy's legs ached and his voice grew tired, but on and on he went until, tucked under the table, he found a hippo with a mean expression on its

face, building a tower with a collection of building bricks.

"That's him. They're mine!" squealed Tabby Kitten pointing first at the hippo and then at the bricks.

Teddy drew himself up to his full height. He looked grand in his red jacket and his wide-brimmed hat. "In the name of the law, I call upon you to give those building bricks back to the person from whom you took them," said Teddy.

The plain, brown, fluffy hippo felt ashamed. He handed the building bricks back to Tabby. "Why did you bother to come after me? Why did you care about silly, little Tabby?" he mumbled to Teddy.

"Teddy Bear Mounties never give up. Teddy Bear Mounties always care about toys who are in the right. Teddy Bear Mounties get their man — or hippo — as the case may be," said Teddy proudly.

After that there was no squabbling or unfairness amongst the toys because they knew Teddy Bear of the Mounties would always see that right was done.

Teddy Bear of the Mounties had many happy years with Darren and several thrilling adventures, too. Sometimes the whole family, with Grandpa, would go for picnics into the wild country places. It was said that on one of the picnics Teddy was seen talking to a white teddy bear he called Snowy, who seemed to be living in the forests, but no one was quite sure. Perhaps that was something Grandpa dreamt while he was dozing after lunch, or perhaps it did happen. Only Teddy and Snowy know.

The Teddy Bears' Picnic

Far, far away, in the heart of a thick forest, is Teddy Bear Land. Some teddy bears live there all their lives. Some bears go away to see the big, wide world. Once a year, in the summer-time, the teddy bears who are living in Teddy Bear land hold a picnic. Not all the bears manage to go. Some are a little too old. Some are a little too young. Some are busy doing housework. Some say they have to stay at home to mow the lawn. Up until a few years ago, the picnics were always arranged by Bossy Boots Bear, who is now retired. They were wonderful picnics and everyone who went enjoyed them.

Bossy Boots was good at arranging the picnics because she loved telling people what to do. "Do this. Do that. And hurry up about it," she would say, as she bustled about getting everything organised.

Some people didn't care for Bossy Boots Bear. They didn't like her loud, jolly voice and they did not like being told what to do.

"We know that Bossy Boots means well and that her heart is in the right place," these bears would say, "but we don't like being ordered about, even when it's for our own good. We like being late, or untidy, or eating between meals, when we are in the mood, without having Bossy Boots saying that we are doing the wrong thing."

Other bears liked Bossy Boots Bear very much.

"If you want a thing done properly, leave it to Bossy Boots," they would say. "Everything is on time when Bossy Boots has anything to do with it."

Whether they liked it or not, everyone in Teddy Bear Land agreed that Bossy Boots was the best bear to organise the yearly Teddy Bears' picnic. With Bossy Boots in charge there were always plenty of sandwiches and cakes and cold drinks for every bear to enjoy. With Bossy Boots in charge, there were always bats and balls to play with and waterproof sheets and cushions to sit on. There were plenty of little packets of sweets for prizes in the races and competitions. There were sacks for the sack race, spoons and hard-boiled eggs for the egg and spoon race. When Bossy Boots Bear shouted in her loud voice, everyone could hear her, so no one missed anything. Best of all, no one dared disobey Bossy Boots, so no one became too excited or too rough, and no one ever dreamt of wandering off and getting lost.

Everyone in Teddy Bear Land agreed that the best picnic Bossy Boots Bear ever arranged was the year of the cheese and cucumber sandwiches. Most bears thought that cheese and cucumber sandwiches were dull, and were none too pleased when they heard that Bossy Boots was preparing them for the picnic. However, Bossy made the sandwiches from her own home-made bread. She grated up the cheese and added a spoonful of salad cream and a pinch of mustard and a blob of

tomato ketchup and cut the cucumber slices very thinly. There was even some talk that she had put grated onions in the sandwiches for the older bears. Everyone loved them.

The bears all met at the Forest Crossroads at half past two in the afternoon. Bossy Boots counted everyone. "Myself and twelve other bears. Quite correct!" she said. "Follow me!"

Pushing along a cart with all the picnic food nicely wrapped and all the things needed for playing games, Bossy Boots led the others to a grassy clearing. They did not walk far so as not to tire the younger bears. Then Bossy told every bear to shake paws with every other bear and say his or her name.

"Now you all know each other, we will play games," said Bossy.

Bossy arranged sack races, egg and spoon races, races for little bears, races for big bears. She arranged competitions for choosing the biggest bear, the smallest bear, the fattest bear, the slimmest bear, the prettiest bear, the toughest bear, the happiest bear and the bear with the longest nose. Bossy Boots arranged the games so that everyone won a prize, for as well as being bossy, she was kind-hearted and clever. Then Bossy handed out bats and balls for the bears to play as they wished

while she set out the food.

Bossy spread a cloth and put out the cheese and cucumber sandwiches, which everyone enjoyed very much. She put out chocolate cakes, biscuits, cartons of jelly, plastic spoons and cartons of drinks. All the bears thanked Bossy Boots and said that no one in Teddy Bear could have arranged things better.

Bossy smiled. "I do like to keep things properly organised," she said.

When the bears had finished eating, they collected up the litter into bags, which Bossy Boots took home to put in her rubbish bin. The pretty, grassy glade looked just as it was before the bears arrived. Then Bossy Boots counted the bears to make sure no one was missing and took them all safely home before she went home and sat down to a well-earned rest.

If you look at the picture of the Teddy Bears' Picnic, you should be able to see Bossy Boots Bear, wearing her smart boots. Count the other bears to see if the twelve that Bossy counted are still there. Try to find the big plate of cheese and cucumber sandwiches, the chocolate cakes and the biscuits and the cartons of jelly and drinks. Can you see the cart Bossy used for taking the food to the picnic? Can you see the bats and the balls? Can you see the path leading home from the grassy glade?

How lucky the teddy bears were to have hard-working Bossy Boots Bear to arrange such a lovely picnic for them. It does seem that, whatever type of person or bear you are, there is a place where you can do well, if only you can find it.

Sailor Teddy

Sailor Teddy lived in Australia. He belonged to a boy named David. Sailor Teddy and David had their home in Sydney and they were both keen on yachting. On Saturdays, Dad would say, "Come along lads, it's off to the marina for us."

Down to the sea the three of them would go, on to their yacht and out into the wide, blue yonder. Not too far out because Mum expected them home for supper, but far enough to have fun.

The other toys envied Sailor Teddy for his adventurous life. He was also admired for his bravery. Whatever happened, Sailor Teddy would stand firm with a calm smile on his face.

"Worse things happen at sea," he'd say. "This is nothing."

Sailor Teddy was so well-known for his courage that David's sisters used to ask for him if they had to do anything that made them feel trembly. The girls had dolls and cuddly rabbits for their favourite toys, and they were wonderful but, when a person needs a staunch companion, a bear seems best.

There was the time that Michelle had to visit the dentist. Mum was going, too, and Michelle quite understood that it was all for her own good so she didn't risk having horrid toothaches later. However, she couldn't bring herself to feel she was looking forward to a fun visit, and she asked David if she could borrow Sailor Teddy to sit in the dentist's waiting room with her.

David was kind enough to agree and the day came when Mum, Michelle and Sailor Teddy were all waiting next to the dentist's surgery in a sunny room with lots of chairs and a table piled with magazines. While Mum looked at a magazine, Michelle and Sailor Teddy snuggled down together and whispered quietly so that they would not annoy any of the other patients.

"This is nothing," said Sailor Teddy, smiling at Michelle from under his sailor hat. "Worse things happen at sea."

"Do they?" replied Michelle. "You and David and Dad always seem happy when you come back from your sailing trips."

"We put a brave face on things," said Sailor Teddy, "and, most of the time, going down to the sea in ships — or yachts — is marvellous, but sometimes it's not. Sailors have scrub the decks and climb up the rigging to the top of the swaying mast to

untangle ropes. Now, Michelle, when you go into that dentist's surgery, he's not going to make you scrub the floor or climb up to the ceiling and hang on to the light shade, is he?"

"No, nothing like that," agreed Michelle.

"There you are," beamed Sailor Teddy. "You're doing well already. And something else — I'm sure there are no Doldrums or Sargasso Seas nor sea monsters in the dentist's either."

"Mum didn't mention anything like that," said Michelle. "She said something about a chair that went up and down."

"Up and down! Up and down!" laughed Sailor Teddy. "No one knows the meaning of up and down until they have sailed over the ocean. I'll tell you about the voyage of Captain Christopher Columbear who left Spain in 1492 to sail the Atlantic Ocean. I believe there was someone called Christopher Columbus who sailed about the same time and discovered America, but I don't know much about that. Anyway, Christopher Columbear was a nice fellow, but he had little money and hoped to make his fortune by sailing far away towards the west, thinking to come to a place called India, which was in the east."

"That seems a strange idea," said Michelle.

"That's what everyone said at the time," replied Sailor Teddy, "because people then thought the world was flat, but if you believe that the world is round then what Christopher Columbear said made sense. If the world is round and you sail far enough to the west, you come round to the east — eventually."

"Sailing west from Spain to reach India didn't make sense when you think that America and China and Malaya and places like that were in the way," said Michelle, who liked looking at maps with Grandpa. Grandpa had travelled the world and had told Michelle a lot about where different countries were.

"But Christopher Columbear didn't know that," explained Sailor Teddy. "It's because of brave sailors like him that we know these things today. Anyway, he sailed his wooden ship west into the setting sun. The waves were huge. Up and down went the little boat. At the top of a high wave, its rudder came out of the water and was useless and, at the bottom, the seas towered over it like mountains. There were no seasick pills in those days. Up — down! Up — down! Everyone felt terrible. Michelle, I don't know why you worry about going up and down in a dentist's chair, much worse things have happened at sea. Anyway, after the storms came the calm. Far out at sea is a place called the Doldrums where no winds blow. Sailing ships can stay in the same place for weeks on end. That happened to Christopher Columbear's ship. The crew were so hungry they ate their shoes. Day after day passed with not a breath of wind.

"At last the captain ordered the longboats to be lowered — ships always carried smaller boats, you know, so that they could row ashore on to shallow beaches.

"Anyway, the longboats were lowered and tied to the ship by ropes and the starving sailors had to row to pull their ships out of the Doldrums into the wind. At last they managed it, the sails filled, and the ship was blown westward again. Then the sailors said they would soon come to the edge of the world and fall off into nothingness and never get home again. People believed things like that in those days. They said that unless Christopher Columbear turned back, they would throw him over the side to feed the fishes and go home without him. Christopher Columbear wasn't afraid. He stood on the bridge of his ship and waved his sword and shouted: 'Avast there, you mutinous seadogs!' That's special sailor-talk, you know."

Michelle interrupted, "Why did he say seadogs? Weren't all the other sailors teddy bears, too?"

"They were a mixed bunch," sniffed Sailor Teddy. "I am sure the loyal crew members were teddy bears, but I am not certain about the others. In any case, anyone who has been at sea for a long time, whether bear or human or cuddly rabbit or whatever, is always called an Old Seadog. Now, where was I? Oh yes. 'Avast there, you mutinous seadogs!' shouted brave Christopher Columbear. 'We will go on sailing westwards or you will hang from the highest yardarm on Portsmouth dockside by order of His Majesty's Lords of the Admiralty in London!'"

Sailor Teddy suddenly paused.

"Wait a minute," he said. "I'm getting my stories mixed up. That was Captain Bligh of the Bounty, who said that. Forget that part of the story. I will tell you about Captain Bligh another time. Worse things happened at sea when he was aboard ship. Now we will get back to Captain Columbear. Christopher

Columbear waved his sword and said that the crew must obey his orders or he would fight them all, one at a time or everyone at once. Christopher was big and his sword was sharp. The crew hesitated. 'But if you obey orders and sail westwards, we shall all be rich and go home and live like kings for the rest of our lives.' said Christopher. The crew looked again at Christopher's sharp sword and decided to give the voyage one more chance.

"On and on westwards the tattered little ship sailed until it came to a stop again. The wind was blowing well and the sails were full, but the ship did not move forwards. Christopher Columbear looked over the side and saw that they were caught up in a sea of floating seaweed! That was a real fright for him, but he did not despair. He sent a small cabin bear who was brave, but who did not pay much attention to his sailing lessons, to the top of the highest mast and told him to look out for clear sea. The mast swayed to and fro and round and round, and the cabin bear was afraid that at any moment he might slip and crash to the deck below or fall into the tangled seaweed. However, like a true teddy bear, he did his duty. Peering through the spray-filled wind he saw clear water to the north. 'Steer left a bit,' he called down to Captain Columbear. 'Now right a bit. Now left again.' Christopher Columbear sighed, 'You would think that after all these weeks at sea he would have learnt that on board ship we call left, port and right, starboard.' He looked up at the top of the mast and shouted through the wailing wind, 'How about saying port and starboard?' 'Anything to please you, captain,' replied the young bear, rather puzzled. 'Port and starboard. Now shall I go on telling you when to turn left and right?' Back on deck Captain Columbear groaned, 'I do my best to teach these youngsters how to talk like proper seamen, but when things like this happen, I think I would rather

be visiting the dentist than sailing as the captain of a ship.' "

"You put that bit in for my sake," said Michelle to Sailor Teddy. "I don't believe Christopher Columbear said that at all."

"After this length of time, who can say?" said Teddy. Then he hurried on with his story. "Eventually they got clear of all the seaweed which nowadays we call the Sargasso Sea. On and on they sailed and at last they landed on an island very near to what we now call America.

"Christopher Columbear and the sailors were delighted. They found fresh water to drink and food to eat and walking along the beach they saw some people. Captain Columbear rushed up to them and said how thrilled he was to be in India and how much he loved their wonderful country and had they got any silks and spices to give him in return for some nice glass beads. You can imagine how disappointed he was when the people told him that the island wasn't India, that they had never heard of India and that they didn't have any silks or spices.

" 'However', the people went on, 'those glass beads look very pretty. Would you think of exchanging them for this yellow stuff which we find lying about in the streams of our island?' The

people showed Christopher Columbear bracelets and earrings made from the yellow stuff, which he knew at once was gold.

'Marvellous!' gasped Christopher. It was one of those fortunate meetings where everyone was pleased. Christopher loaded his ship with water, food and gold, bought in exchange for the glass beads. The island people played happily with the beads, glad to be rid of the gold, which they did not value. In a few days Captain Columbear and his shipmates were sailing home.

"Folk do say it was within a week or two of this that Christopher Columbus landed on the same island and was disappointed, not only because it wasn't India but because he found no gold there either. However, that is the way life goes. Some folk are lucky and some folk are not."

"Did the ship get stuck in the Doldrums or the Sargasso Sea on the way home?" asked Michelle.

"Fortunately not," smiled Sailor Teddy, "but as they were sailing away from the island, and before they reached the deep ocean, a huge sea monster came swimming alongside the ship. It had a small head at the end of a very long neck and its body was enormous. It was almost as big as the ship itself. The sailors

were frightened and they didn't know what to do. They stood along the rail of the ship staring at the terrible creature. The lashing of the monster's tail as it smashed through the water made the ship rock like a toy boat.

"Standing with the rest of the crew was the brave little cabin bear who had climbed to the top of the mast in the Sargasso Sea. He knew the captain was annoyed with him for calling left and right instead of port and starboard and he wanted to do something to get back into favour. Looking round the deck, he saw an empty bottle and picking it up, he threw it hard at the sea monster. 'SHOOO!' he shouted bravely. The whole ship's crew held its breath in horror, wondering if the sea monster would be angry and attack them. Actually the monster was as puzzled by the ship as the sailors were by him. The people of the island had so far invented only small canoes and the monster had never seen a big ship before. He thought it was another sea monster.

"When the bottle hit the sea monster on the head, he thought, 'This fellow is obviously unfriendly. I might as well go away.' With that he dived under the waves and was seen no more. 'Well done!' said Captain Columbear to the little cabin bear and was not annoyed with him any more. The rest of the trip home was

trouble-free. Captain Christopher Columbear landed his ship in a quiet cove and the gold was shared out fairly between him and the crew and they went to their homes and lived happily ever after."

Sailor Teddy looked at Michelle. "When you have gained a fortune in gold, it is wise to keep quiet about it," he said. "People can be very jealous. I believe that Christopher Columbus told everyone who would listen about his discoveries and got himself into a great deal of trouble."

At that moment a lady in a white coat said it was time for

Mum to take Michelle in to see the dentist.

"Now remember," hissed Sailor Teddy, "in that surgery there are no rolling waves to make you seasick, no Doldrums, no Sargasso Seas, no sea monsters. No one is going to make you eat your shoes. If those sailors could find the courage to face all the hardships of a voyage to the ends of the world, surely you can face a little thing like a visit to the dentist."

Michelle squeezed Teddy's paw and went through to the next room.

The dentist was a nice lady, rather like Michelle's grandma.

"Now, you aren't feeling nervous, are you?" she asked.

"No," smiled Michelle. "Worse things happen at sea!"

Xenophon Bear's March to the Sea

Autumn was almost over. The first snows of the cold, northern winter were blowing in the air. There was time for one last group of teddy bears to leave Teddy Bear Land and make the dangerous journey through the dark forests to join Father Christmas in his home near the North Pole.

The big sledge pulled by young reindeer and driven by an elf had come hurtling down the narrow trail. Gratefully, the elf and reindeer had hurried into the big hut kept ready for them on the northern side of Teddy Bear Land. They rested and ate and warmed themselves before the big log fire, and the elf driver told the group of waiting teddy bears to waste no time in loading the sledge for the return journey.

"Winter seems to be coming early this year," said the elf, who was a reliable worker and helped Father Christmas with the preparations for his Christmas journeys. "Terrible gales blew as we came down here and I'm sure I heard trees crashing down on the trail behind us. If I'm right, we shall have to clear them on our journey back or we shall never get through. I heard packs of wolves howling and there were herds of caribou on the move. I tell you, I didn't like the look of things. If you teddies would rather not risk the journey, I'll make a quick dash back alone and tell Father Christmas you'll be coming up next spring to be delivered as presents the Christmas after this. He'll understand."

The teddy bears looked at each other.

"I think we must go this year," said Xenophon, one of the little group, "we don't like to let Father Christmas down and we

had set our hearts on being in Greece this Christmas."

The teddy bears who went up to Father Christmas Land could usually choose which country they should go to as Christmas presents.

"Greece, eh?" said the elf. "A very nice place, so I hear. I suppose you want to go there because of all the ancient ruins. You want to improve your education."

"Not exactly," said Xenophon, "although I'm sure all that is very interesting. The truth is, a teddy friend, who is already in Greece, sent word back by the driver of the coach which takes teddies to the shops, that the honey and the honey cakes and the home-made toffee with seeds in it, and some special yoghurt and something called moussaka, which they make there, are absolutely delicious. We thought we would like to go there and try them. I gave myself the name of Xenophon, which was the name of a brave Greek soldier, to get us into the right spirit, and here we are ready to go."

"Very well then, but you know the risks," said the elf. "We will go as soon as the reindeer are properly rested. They are only young animals being trained for the big Christmas flights. We cannot expect too much of them."

The journey north to Father Christmas Land was supposed to be made in one long rush without stopping. It lasted a day and a night and a day, and was very tiring. To some, it might have seemed more sensible for the bears to stop and camp for a night's rest along the way, but stopping in that forest was more dangerous than going on. The wolves were hungry. The Arctic foxes were fierce. The forests were dense and one trail looked like another. More than one teddy bear who ventured into the northlands had been lost and never seen again.

The brave band of teddy bears, with the elf as their leader, loaded the sledge with the usual presents from Teddy Bear Land for Father and Mrs Christmas. They put aboard food for the journey and extra rations in case they were delayed. They packed warm clothing, tents to camp should the sledge be wrecked, matches to light camp fires and big sticks in case the wolves or anything else attacked.

"Of course, we hope none of this ever happens, but in the forest it is better to be safe than sorry," said the elf.

The bears had already filled out the correct forms and made the proper arrangements for leaving. They called their last goodbyes, climbed into the sledge and headed north.

Soon the lights of Teddy Bear Land were hidden round a bend in the track. The dark trees closed about them. The narrow trail curved ahead. The only sounds were the thudding of the hooves of the reindeer, the puffing and panting of their breath, and the rasp of the sledge runners over the mud and the tree roots.

For several hours everything went well. The teddy bears started to chat together and make jokes about whether any of the reindeer which pulled Father Christmas' sledge at Christmas really did have red noses. They came across several fallen trees and had to stop, but the elf knew what to do. He had made the journey many times.

"Xenophon! Pick up this big stick and take two teddies to keep guard," he said. "Pink Teddy! Hold the heads of the reindeer so they don't run away. The rest of you help me to roll the tree to the side of the track."

With a few grunts and cries of "HEAVE-HO!" the work was done. The bears scrambled back on the sledge and away they raced.

When three trees had been cleared and evening was approaching, the elf smiled at Xenophon. "I think the worst might be over," he said. "We're through the part of the forest where the gales were blowing. There should be no more fallen trees and I haven't heard any wolf packs, have you?"

Xenophon opened his mouth to reply, but never got as far as speaking. A huge caribou with mighty horns crashed across the trail, missing the reindeer by a whisker. It was enough to terrify the young animals. They reared and broke half their reins, then bolted down a side trail which had been made by wild animals and did not lead to Father Christmas Land at all. The sledge swayed from side to side, spilling boxes and baskets as it went. On the bears rocked, for miles, until the reins broke completely and the reindeer ran away. The sledge was overturned and the teddies, with what was left of their supplies, were thrown higgledy piggledy amongst the trees. The elf banged his head on a rock and, when he sat up he couldn't remember a thing.

Xenophon stood up dizzily and, groping into the overturned

sledge, found a box of matches and tucked it into his pocket. Then he rounded up all the teddy bears. They were bruised and shaken, but no one was badly hurt. No one but the elf.

"Where am I?" he said. "Who am I? Who are you?"

The teddies looked at him in dismay. The elf was the only one who knew the way. He was their leader and he was no use at all.

"We must choose a new leader," said Pink Teddy. "I vote for Xenophon. Let Xenophon be our leader and do his best to get us safely to Father Christmas Land."

"Yes! Xenophon! Xenophon!" chorused the other bears.

"Who is Xenophon? Who are you? Who am I?" rambled the elf.

Xenophon looked round at the darkening sky. In the distance he had heard the sound of howling wolves. The first task was to get safely through the night.

"Collect branches and thorn twigs and make a barricade all round us," he said. "Collect wood to make a fire in the centre of the barricade. Collect as much as you can of the things which have fallen from the sledge."

The bears raced about and, by night-time, they were sitting round a huge roaring fire, and protecting them was a barricade of branches twisted together with thorn bushes. Xenophon patted the box of matches in his pocket. While he could make a roaring fire, they all stood a chance of getting through.

Xenophon and the biggest bears spoke together. They had all heard stories of the journey to Father Christmas Land and they collected together their little bits of knowledge. By the time dawn broke, Xenophon knew what he had to do.

"We are all agreed that the usual trail to Father Christmas Land leads straight north until it reaches the open, melted sea water surrounding the island where Father Christmas lives," he said. "Elves and canoes are waiting there and, if we reach them,

we shall be safe. Teddy Bears, we must march north to the sea!"

"Agreed!" cheered the bears. They collected all the food and warm clothes they could carry. They took the bags of presents for Father and Mrs Christmas because they didn't wish to arrive seeming like bears of no importance. They looked up at the sun to find where north was and they started on their long march.

The stronger bears carried sticks and walked on the outside. The smaller bears carried supplies and led the elf along on the inside of the group. They marched for hours. They marched for days. Whizzing along in a sledge is one thing. Trudging in a group, carrying heavy loads and leading a sick elf, is quite another. But the teddies, led by Xenophon, never thought of giving up. They were true companions and helped each other when they were tired or their paws were sore. At night they built huge fires and barricades of thorn branches. The wolves prowled and howled all around, but they didn't dare to come close. Then one dawn a young fox cub came sniffing round the camp.

"What are you teddy bears doing here?" he yipped to a young bear. "I usually see you roaring along on a sledge. I have never seen any of you marching through the forest before. Do you need any help?"

"Oh, yes PLEASE!" smiled the young teddy. "We are lost. Can you show us the way to the sea, the part where the elves and canoes wait to ferry people across to Father Christmas Island?"

"Of course!" yipped the fox cub. "Follow me."

He paused. "I suppose you will give me a present if I help you? Have you any nice things with you?"

"Yes, we have," beamed the young teddy. "We have some lovely presents for Father and Mrs Christmas. I am sure Xenophon will unpack a few and give them to you, if you help us. Won't you Xenophon?"

The young teddy called Xenophon over and told him all that the fox cub had said. To his surprise Xenophon looked cross, but he thanked the cub and said if he led them to the right part of the coast, he would be rewarded with a warm blanket to keep him cosy at night. Off they set on another day's march, but Xenophon went from teddy to teddy whispering, "We do not know whether or not we can trust this fox cub. Follow him but watch him. Be more careful than ever. He may be leading us into a trap.

Then Xenophon pulled the young teddy aside.

"Never tell a stranger such things again," he said. "Never tell a stranger that we have lots of nice presents with us. Why should a fox be a friend to us? We are strangers to him. Perhaps he is helping us because he is kind. Perhaps he is in league with grown-up foxes, who plan to rob us. Be extra careful!"

So the teddy bears marched, half hopeful and half more fearful than ever. As afternoon dragged on, when all the bears were weary and some were wondering if they could carry on or would have to drop by the wayside, they started walking up a steep hill.

One strong bear, carrying a big stick, was walking ahead as a lookout. He reached the crest of the hill first. Suddenly he started dancing about and shouting and waving his arms. Xenophon, and those a little way behind him, were alarmed and thought he was being attacked. They ran forward to help him.

As soon as they reached the top of the hill they started shouting and laughing and pointing, too. Those coming up behind them longed to know what they could see, but they dared not drop their supplies. Holding tight to their precious food and clothes and leading the elf, they clambered up the slope as fast as they could. At last they heard what the others were shouting.

"THE SEA! THE SEA!" the teddies were calling. "Look down there. There are the huts and canoes and the elves. There is the sea and on the other side is Father Christmas Island. We have marched to the sea. We are safe!"

They all hugged and kissed each other. They made a big pile of rocks to mark the spot where they had first seen the sea. They thanked the fox cub, who it seems had been a friend after all, and they gave him the warm blanket they had promised. They ran down the slope and spoke to the elves, who told them that the young reindeer had found their way home days before. Then they all had a big supper together. As night fell the fox club slipped away into the forest with his blanket, back to his own kind.

The next day the elves paddled the teddies across to the safe, warm home of Father Christmas. When he heard their story he patted Xenophon Bear and said, "I am sure the real Xenophon would have been proud of you."

After a few weeks the elf became better and at Christmas all the teddies were safely delivered to homes in Greece.

Loch Ness Teddy

Loch Ness is the largest lake in a country called Scotland. The lake is over thirty kilometres long, but quite narrow. Tall dark mountains glower down from one side, but a strip of flatter land, with a road, runs along the other shore. Loch Ness is dark and murky. Many streams and several rivers carry peat and bits of bracken and fallen trees to sink or float in the cold water. Anyone who tries to peer down into Loch Ness does not succeed. After a few metres all is swirling blackness.

None of this worried Loch Ness Teddy. Teddy bears rarely go swimming, so the fact that Loch Ness was cold and made black by rotting peat was neither here nor there to him.

"The loch is beautiful," he would smile, "I love living here."

Loch Ness Teddy's home was a small cottage on the shore of the lake. He belonged to Angus, a fine Scottish lad, who was old enough to go to school. Every day Loch Ness Teddy sat in the window of the cottage, where he could see both Loch Ness and the path which led up to the road. Teddy would watch for Angus to come home from school and he would doze a little and look out over the rippling waters.

"I cannot understand why Teddy's side seams have come unstitched," said Angus' mother. "When Angus was at home all day and playing with Teddy I could have understood if Teddy became worn out, but he didn't. It's only since he has been sitting still at the window all day that these stitches have pulled apart. Tomorrow I must mend him, but why his seams have split is a real mystery."

Toy Shaggy Dog, who belonged to Angus' little sister Heather, glanced at Loch Ness Teddy and smiled. He knew why Teddy's stitches had come undone. Heather did not yet go to school, therefore Toy Shaggy Dog did not sit in the window looking out at the path and the loch. He was busy playing with Heather or sitting in front of the fire, as dogs love to do, but Toy Shaggy Dog knew that during all those long hours while Teddy watched from the window, he saw things which other people did not see.

"Any sign of Nessie today?" woofed Toy Shaggy Dog, when

NESSIE?

Mum and Heather were out of the room.

"No," replied Teddy, "but I expect to see her soon. It's several days since she last came for a chat and she must be wanting to hear the latest news."

All was quiet in the cottage. Mum and Heather were away in the kitchen knitting, while they waited for some scones to cook. The only sound was the lapping of the lake on the small beach a few steps from the window where Teddy sat. Suddenly there was a swirling as a large shape rose from the deeper water. A small head on a very long neck rose up high and looked around. Satisfied that no one but Teddy was watching, the Loch Ness Monster waddled from the water.

"Good afternoon, Teddy," she said. "Have you anything to tell me?"

"Good afternoon, Niseag," replied Teddy. Niseag was the monster's real name and she did not like to be called anything else. It was an old Gaelic name, hundreds of years old, like Nessie herself. "There is some news," went on Teddy. "Next week the school term finishes and there will be lots of families visiting the area for their summer holidays, camping by the loch and fishing and taking photographs, but you know that. I am merely reminding you. The news about the important matter which worries you so much is bad I am afraid. That rich pop-singer who is determined to find you has been given permission to make what they call sonar soundings all across the loch. According to last night's television news he will be ready in two months' time."

The Loch Ness Monster groaned.

"That means no peace for weeks," she complained. "There will be nothing but noise and people and upset. The whole lake will be churned up so that I cannot see where I am going. Finding my way amongst all that floating peat is difficult enough at the best of times. Feeding will be almost impossible, too. All the commotion drives the fish away, especially the salmon. Last time they had one of those sonar scans of the loch I became as thin as a rake, what with being too upset to eat and not being able to find any food anyway."

The Loch Ness Monster was a hunter and a meat eater, something which a lot of people thought was not nice, but as

Teddy always said, "Nobody is perfect and you have to take people as you find them."

"I don't mind the ordinary holiday-makers," said Nessie, "I can stay away from them and go to the lonely parts of the loch, but these television and scientific people with their sonar rays and video cameras really upset me. It is only a few weeks since the last lot went away."

The Loch Ness Monster stayed chatting with Teddy for several more minutes, asking how Angus was getting on at school and enquiring if Heather had learnt to tell left from right yet. Then she turned and waddled back into the loch on her four flippers. There was a splashing and some spray was thrown into the air as she thrashed her tail from side to side and finally sank from sight.

Toy Shaggy Dog looked up at Teddy. "Nessie chats to you happily enough," he said. "Why does she want to avoid everyone else?"

"She gives all sorts of excuses," replied Teddy, "but I think there are actually two real reasons. She thinks that if any of these scientific people discover her they might take her away to live in a big tank somewhere and keep studying her all the time. You can understand that she would not like that. Who would? The other reason is that — how can I put this without being unkind? — Nessie is not the most beautiful creature in the world."

Toy Shaggy Dog laughed. "You mean, as I have often heard Grandma say, the Loch Ness Monster was not standing in the front row when good looks were handed out!"

"Exactly," agreed Teddy. "Her feelings have been badly hurt. It all started back in the year 565 when Saint Colomba came over here from Ireland. One of his followers was swimming in the lake, when Nessie, or Niseag, as everyone called her in those days, thought that this man was an extra big salmon and came up and tried to eat him. The lake was a very lonely place in those days and, although Niseag saw people walking along the bank, she hardly ever saw men swimming. Apparently, Saint Colomba and others came dashing out in a boat and shouted and waved their arms and Niseag though they had taken a dislike to her and swam away. She was particularly upset because she felt that a saint of all people should have forgiven a genuine mistake.

"For years after that Nessie stayed away from people, but in 1933 she slipped ashore to find a rabbit for supper and was hurrying back to the loch with it, minding her own business and bothering no one, except the rabbit of course, when a man and his wife came driving along the road. How they squealed at the sight of Nessie! They stopped the car and shrieked out that she was an ugly monster. Nessie was deeply offended."

"But she is an ugly monster," barked Toy Shaggy Dog.

"That may be," said Teddy, "but she does not like people to say so. Again, she kept to herself as much as she could, but with cameras becoming cheap, even poor fishermen living by Loch Ness could afford them. Soon photographs of Nessie appeared in the newspapers. Imagine how Nessie felt when, as she was swimming below the surface of the loch, she heard people on the shore or in boats saying that the photographs of her were really of floating tree trunks. She was so upset that she decided she never wanted her photograph taken again. Nor did she want the whole world seeing how ugly she was or saying she was so thick-looking she must be a tree trunk."

"I can understand all that," agreed Toy Shaggy Dog. "If I were Nessie, I expect I should want to hide away from people as well. I suppose she comes up to talk to you because you sit quietly and have no camera."

"Yes," smiled Teddy. "She saw me sitting here watching for

Angus to come home from school and she thought that as I lived in a cottage with a television, I would hear the news about scientific search parties coming to the loch. She asked me if I would give her warning when they were due to arrive. I agreed. We fell to chatting about this and that and we have been friends ever since."

"I wonder if Mother will ever guess why the seams down your sides have split?" woofed Toy Shaggy Dog.

"I can't say," smiled Teddy. "I really do try not to split my sides laughing, but I can't help it. I know, as you do Shaggy Dog, that the best and only way to see the Loch Ness Monster is to leave your camera at home and to sit quietly at the side of the lake until she feels like coming over for a chat. When I see these television crews and these scientific people, with cameras slung all over them and sonar beams everywhere, swarming about in their dozens; when I see them arriving in brightly painted coaches, talking at the tops of their voices, followed by hot, noisy vans which serve them food during all those breaks they keep having from work; when I see all that, as I did a few weeks ago, I am afraid I do split my sides laughing. I know they will never see Nessie. They are doing everything wrong. Nessie is hiding from them deep in the black depths of Loch Ness and good luck to her. That's what I say."

"Yes, I wish her luck too," agreed Toy Shaggy Dog.

Bedtime Story Bear

Bedtime Story Bear or B.S.B. for short, was a cuddly, snuggly teddy bear. He wasn't too big or too small. He loved listening to bedtime stories. B.S.B. never yawned or interrupted whoever was telling the story. He never said things like, "I've heard that bit before. It's boring! Hurry along to the next part" or "You've missed something out because you want to go downstairs and watch television. Cinderella's Ugly Sisters tried the glass slipper on before Cinderella. I know that. You can't fool me."

No, whatever bedtime story he heard, while he was tucked up in bed with his owner, B.S.B. appreciated it.

Some of the other toys spent the night in the bedroom and listened to the bedtime stories, too. However, many of them fell asleep half way through. Other toys were left downstairs in the games room or the toy cupboard and heard nothing.

So it was on days when the family were out and the toys were downstairs together, that the others would turn to Bedtime Story Bear and say, "B.S.B. tell us a story."

"With pleasure," B.S.B. would say. "Now let me think. I told you about Red Riding Hood last week and I know it's not long since we were talking about Puss in Boots. What a clever cat he was! I shouldn't like to have had cross words with him!"

One afternoon Bedtime Story Bear smiled and said, "A few days ago, Mother read out a story about a bear."

Bedtime Story Bear glanced down modestly and went on, "I know I shouldn't say it, but I do find bear stories the best of all."

The other toys were quiet. Dolly thought stories about dolls were best and Pink Pig thought stories about pigs were best and Big Elephant thought stories about elephants were best. They didn't say a thing, because they didn't wish to upset B.S.B.

"I'm sure your bear story will be thrilling," said Dolly. "Please do go on, B.S.B."

"The story was called Snow White and Rose Red," said B.S.B.

At once Pink Pig interrupted. "I know the story of Snow White," he grunted, "it's about Snow White and seven dwarfs, but I don't remember any Rose Red or any bears."

"That is a different story," explained B.S.B. "Mother's story

was about Snow White and Rose Red, and a bear, too."

This is the story Bedtime Story Bear told to the other toys.

Long ago, at the edge of a forest, a woman lived in a cottage with her two daughters. In the garden of the cottage was a rose bush which bore lovely red roses. When the first girl was born, with red hair, the mother thought she was as beautiful as the roses in the garden, so she called her Rose Red. When the second, very fair girl, was born, the mother thought she was as beautiful as the white snows of winter and she called her Snow White.

The years passed and the girls grew to be beautiful young women. One bitterly cold winter's evening as they sat by the fire, spinning wool to be made into cloth, a knock came at the door.

"Open the door, Rose Red," said her mother, "that must be a traveller caught in the forest and seeking shelter from the wind."

Rose Red opened the door and thought she saw a tall man in

a fur coat. She stood aside and invited him to come in. To the terror of the three women, a huge bear stepped into the room. Snow White and Rose Red screamed and hid behind the bed which, as they were poor folk, was in the one living room.

"Don't be afraid," said the bear. "I will not harm you. I am cold and I should like to warm myself by your fire."

The mother, who had seen more of the world than her daughters, knew that any bear who could speak must be a better sort of creature than the wild bears which lived in the deep forest.

"Come in and warm yourself by the fire and welcome," she said, "but take care you do not singe your fur."

The bear quietly settled by the fire and, after a while, Snow White and Rose Red crept from their hiding place. They brushed the snow and tangles from the bear's fur and he thanked them politely. Soon they were good friends. The bear slept by the fire for the night and did no harm to anyone.

In the morning the girls let the bear out of the cottage and he went into the forest. Every evening of that cold winter, the bear came to the home of Snow White and Rose Red to sleep before the fire, and every morning he went away to roam through the forest.

Then one morning, in the springtime, the bear said to Snow

White, "I shall not come back to the cottage this evening. I have some treasure hidden in an underground cave. In the winter, when the ground is frozen, it is safe. Now the snows are melting, the wicked dwarfs who live in the forest will try to find my treasure and steal it. I must guard it day and night."

The bear glanced through the cottage door and saw that the sun was shining warmly and that the snow was melting.

"I may have stayed here too long already," he growled anxiously, and leaping to his feet rushed through the doorway, tearing his fur on the door knocker as he went.

Snow White thought that underneath, where the fur was torn, was glittering gold cloth. The girls missed the bear, who had been like a pet dog to them. However, he was gone, and that was that.

A few days later, the mother sent the girls into the forest to gather firewood. As they passed a fallen tree, they saw a dwarf with a long beard. The beard was caught in a crack in the tree. Struggle as he might, the dwarf could not pull free. When he saw Snow White and Rose Red, he called to them. "Hurry up and release my beard. I've better things to do than wait here."

The girls thought the dwarf could have asked in a more polite way, as indeed he should have, but being kind-hearted they went to help him in spite of his rudeness. They pulled and tugged at the beard, but it was so deep in the tree they could not get it out.

"How did you get your beard caught in the tree?" gasped Snow White in amazement.

"If it's any business of yours, which it isn't," snapped the dwarf, "I was driving a wedge into the tree in order to split it for firewood, but the wedge slipped and the tree snapped shut with my beard trapped in the middle. Now stop wasting time and get the beard out, you two stupid good-for-nothings!"

By this time Snow White and Rose Red were fed up with the dwarf, but in spite of his sharp talk they could not leave him trapped. Snow White remembered she had a pair of scissors. She used them to cut off the part of the beard caught in the tree and freed the dwarf. Instead of thanking the girls, he shouted at them more than ever, complaining that they had spoilt his handsome beard. He pulled a large bag of gold from beneath the tree and ran off without offering the girls any reward for their help.

The next week their mother sent the girls to catch fish for

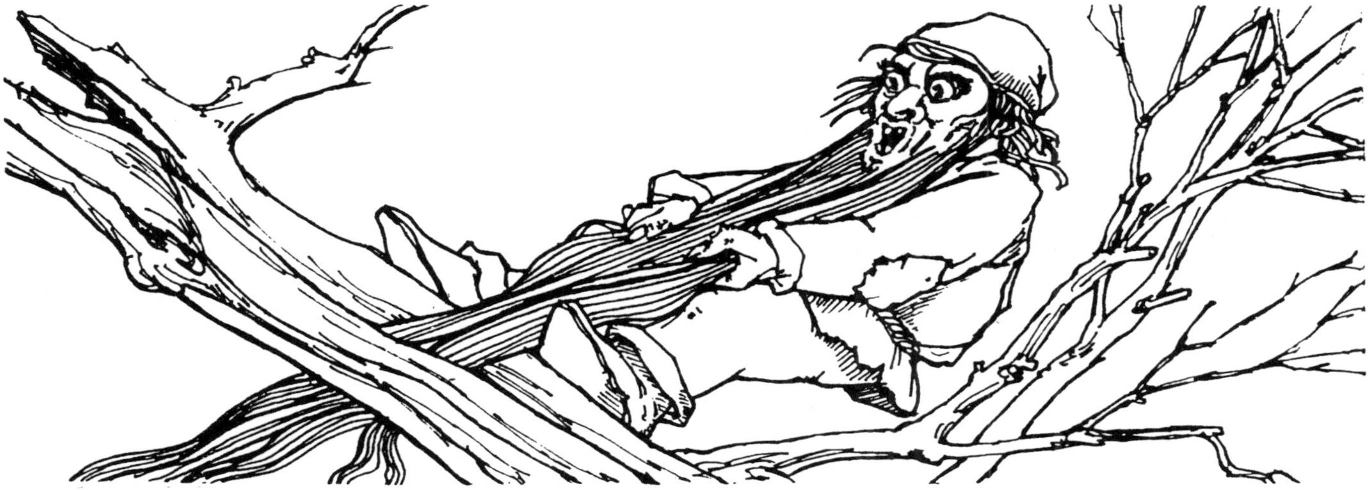

supper. As they walked towards a stream, they saw the same horrid dwarf leaping up and down at the water's edge.

"I wonder why he's jumping about like that?" said Rose Red.

Immediately the dwarf heard her voice, he called, "Come and help me. Can't you see I am in trouble, you stupid girl?"

Snow White and Rose Red ran to the stream and looked into the clear water. There, a large fish, hook and line with which the dwarf had been fishing and the dwarf's beard were all tangled together. As the fish darted to and fro, he kept dragging the dwarf into the water. The dwarf leapt up and down, trying to get free, but he couldn't untangle his beard and he hadn't the strength to pull the large fish on to the bank of the stream.

"You are in trouble!" gasped Rose Red.

"I don't need telling that!" screamed the dwarf. "Untangle my beard and stop gossiping."

Again the girls thought the dwarf did not deserve help, but seeing that the little fellow would soon be pulled under the water, Snow White once more took her scissors from her pocket and snipping off part of the beard, set the dwarf free.

He was furious. He screamed at the girls that if they damaged his beautiful beard again, he would complain to their mother. Then he picked up a bag of pearls from the bed of the stream and disappeared behind a rock.

Needless to say, the girls never wished to see the ungrateful dwarf again, but a few weeks later, on their way to do some shopping in the village, they saw a huge eagle swoop down on the dwarf as he was about to enter a cave. The girls ran forward and grabbed at the dwarf's coat as he was being taken up into the air. After a great tug-of-war with the eagle, they pulled the dwarf free and the eagle flew away. Once more, instead of being

grateful, the dwarf complained that the girls should have freed him without tearing his coat. Turning his back, he carried a bag of precious stones down into his cave.

Coming home from shopping, the girls passed the same cave. There was the dwarf with his gold, pearls and precious stones spread out on the ground. They were about to hurry on, when the dwarf saw them.

"Spying on me, are you?" he shouted. "Trying to rob me of my treasure, are you?"

Seizing a stick, the horrid dwarf started to beat the girls. As they screamed, there was a loud growl and a huge bear ran from amongst the trees. Snow White and Rose Red were more frightened than ever, until they recognised their old friend who had slept by their fire all through the winter. The bear ran towards the dwarf, who immediately shouted that the bear should spare him and eat the girls.

"They are young and will taste much better than me," said the dwarf.

"Long have I searched for you," said the bear. "Now I will deal with you and end your wicked ways for ever."

He struck the dwarf a mighty blow with his paw and the dwarf never moved again. As the girls stared at the bear, they saw his fur fall aside and a handsome prince dressed in a suit of gold stood before them.

"I am a prince," said. "This dwarf put a curse on me that I should roam the forest as a bear until his death released me from his spell. Then he stole my treasure, but now he is dead and I am free to take my riches and return to my family."

The prince, knowing the correct way to behave, escorted Snow White and Rose Red safely to their home. He gave their mother some of the treasure to thank her for her kindness all through the cold winter. Then he returned to his royal palace. A few weeks later he and his brother came to visit Snow White and Rose Red. The prince, who had been a bear, asked Snow White to marry him and his brother proposed to Rose Red. So they married and lived happily ever after in comfort and plenty.

"Thank you Bedtime Story Bear. That was an exciting tale," said the other toys.

"And there was one dwarf in it," smiled Pink Pig, "so I was partly right."

Big Elephant looked hard at Bedtime Story Bear. "Do you think you might turn into a handsome prince one day, like the bear in the story?" he asked.

B.S.B. looked up in surprise and it almost seemed that a tear came into his eye.

"Don't you like me as I am?" he asked.

Dolly spoke hastily. She hated to see anyone's feelings hurt.

"Of course we like you as you are," she said. "Why I'm sure if the bear in the story had been a teddy bear and not a wild bear, Snow White and Rose Red would much rather have kept him as a teddy than have him turn into the most handsome prince in the world. Everyone knows that teddy bears are wonderful. TEDDY BEARS FOREVER! That's what I say."

All the other toys cheered and clapped and Bedtime Story Bear smiled a happy smile.

"Thank you," he said, "We teddies do our best to please everyone."